A Brighter Day:
How Parents Can Help African
American Youth

Gail L. Thompson, Ph.D.

African American Images

Dedication

This book is dedicated to my late siblings, Tammy, Jeffery, and Calvin, my outstanding role model and late grandmother Francis Johnson, and to my nieces Dr. TreaAndrea Marie Russworm, LaShunda Hadnot, Tiffany Hadnot, Shaunte Hadnot, Angel Davis, Elyse' Cheatum, and Jayda Moore, and my nephews JaCory Hadnot, R.J. Young—Rashaed Young Jr, Paul Davis, and Matty Davis.

A Brighter Day:
How Parents Can Help African American Youth
Acknowledgments

First of all, I want to thank God for giving me the idea to write this book nearly 20 years ago. In spite of the fact that many editors, publishers, and literary agents didn't believe that it was worth publishing, and many sent me rejection letters, I continued to believe in this project anyway.

I'm grateful to my husband, Rufus, and children, Nafissa, NaChe', and Stephen, my son-in-law, Derrick Spires, my sister Sergeant Tracy Harkless, and mentor Dr. David E. Drew, and colleagues Dr. Lourdes Arguelles, Dr. Barbara DeHart, Dr. Delacy Ganley, Dr. Anita Quintinar, and Lisa Loop for continuing to believe in the work that I do. I am also extremely grateful to Dr. Jawanza Kunjufu for all of his contributions to the African American "community," not only through the books that he has authored and presentations that he gives throughout the nation, but also by giving other authors a chance to be published. Thank you, Dr. Kunjufu for believing in *A Brighter Day* and for agreeing to publish it.

Furthermore, I would like to thank my good friends Betty Coleman Esq, Malinda West, Cynthia Hebron, Deborah Tavasti, and Dr. Angela Louque for their sage advice, prayers, and friendship. Dr. James Comer, Dr. William Hammond, and the late Dr. Asa Hilliard are three of the most supportive African American scholars whom I have ever had the honor of knowing. My mother Velma Coleman; cousins Bobbie Timberlake, Carolyn Clemmons, Debbie Jo Crear, and Carolyn Pickney; aunts Dorothy Taylor, Linda Price, Wilma Hester, Annie Ruth Palmer, Lillian Mitchell, Glennis Johnson, Lisa Johnson, and Ebbie Crear; and uncles Leonard Frank Johnson, Reverend J.D. Palmer, Reverend Jesse Mitchell, and

Acknowledgments

Bishop John Hester have made it clear to me that they are proud of my accomplishments.

I would also like to thank literary agents Audra Barrett, who was excited about this book, and Marie Brown, who sent me a very encouraging letter about the book.

Last but definitely not least, I would like to thank the women of Mt. Sinai Church of God in Christ, my friend Pamela Battle who read the longer version of this book, Evangelist Althea Sims, and the members of Good Samaritan AME Church, especially Pastor Jackie Williams, for believing that this book should be published and for praying for its future.

A Brighter Day:
How Parents Can Help African American Youth
Contents

Introduction: For a Child's Sake

In 2005, I met an unemployed, biracial (half-Black, half-White) woman who was in a rut that she claimed she didn't know how to escape. Her three young children had been fathered by three different Black men to whom she'd never been married. The woman was currently living with the father of her youngest child, and even though he treated her one-year-old son "well," by all accounts, he mistreated his "baby mama." Two individuals told me that he made her work as a prostitute, an allegation the woman denied to me. However, she did admit that he beat her regularly, often knocked her down, choked her, and hit her on the head. Her boyfriend was also so controlling that he told her how to dress, where she could and couldn't go, and with whom she could associate. He frequently threatened to throw her out on the street. Sometimes, the beatings occurred in front of her two youngest children: the man's one-year-old son, and a three-year-old girl who had a different father. However, because she believed that she had nowhere else to go, the woman tolerated the abuse. Thankfully, her oldest child, a six-year-old boy, did not witness this brutality, for he lived in another state with his father.

During the previous year, after a particularly brutal beating, the young mother had taken drastic action by calling the police and filing charges against her abusive boyfriend. She got a restraining order, and while he was in jail, she grabbed her daughter and escaped to a shelter for battered women. Believing that her one-year-old son would be well cared for, she left him behind with her boyfriend's parents.

During her months of "freedom," the woman and her daughter had a rough time. They lived in a shelter and then in

A Brighter Day:
How Parents Can Help African American Youth

a motel for a short while. Later, for nearly two months, the little girl was sent to live with her biological father (who resented being stuck with a child he didn't want to be bothered with) and the child's great grandmother.

After the woman's abusive boyfriend got out of jail, she went back to the same situation from which she'd escaped. "I stayed with him," she later told me, "because I felt he was a good father to his son." When I replied, "A good father wouldn't beat his child's mother," she agreed but claimed that it had taken her some time to realize this. I told her what Gavin DeBecker, "the nation's leading expert on predicting violence,"[1] said: ". . . I believe that the first time a woman is hit, she is a victim and the second time, she is a volunteer."[2] DeBecker also said, "Children learn most from modeling, and as a mother accepts the blows, so likely will her daughter. As a father delivers the blows, so likely will his son."[3] Indeed this was true, for the woman's little girl had already begun to imitate what she'd witnessed between her mother and the mother's boyfriend. On at least two occasions, the child had been caught choking herself until her face turned red.

That year, during our numerous conversations, I heard many stories from this mother. The comments that bothered me the most were, "I don't even know how to get out of this situation. I don't even know where to start." So, I suggested that she begin reading self-help books and books about individuals who overcame challenges to learn how they did it. She said she'd never even thought of this but believed it was good advice. When I suggested that she start searching for a job, she seemed receptive. When I said she should consider going to a community college in order to further her education and thereby increase her chances of getting higher-paying jobs, she seemed to take my words seriously (although I later learned that she didn't have a G.E.D. or a high school diploma). She even appeared receptive to my suggestion that she start taking parenting classes. Because she had spent some of her own childhood in foster care, and she had a rocky relationship with her mother, she agreed that this could help her break a negative cycle.

Unfortunately, I learned that this woman knew all the right things to say and at times, would even follow through on her promises. But she kept going back to her abusive boyfriend and getting into more trouble. In 2006, during a heated conversation, I told her that her decisions and actions were hurting her three children and that she needed to make *their* well-being her top priority. Initially she chose to ignore my advice, for when I first started writing this book the situation had worsened. The woman's boyfriend, not her children, was still her top priority. Catering to his needs and wishes was more important to her than doing what was best for her children.

In late 2006, after being abandoned in a motel, the woman's little girl was placed in the custody of Child Protective Services. But the story has a happy ending. Evidently this was the wake-up call that this mother needed. In order to get her child back, she completed a court-ordered residential drug treatment program, took parenting classes, and started seeing a therapist regularly. Today she is working full-time. She has custody of her daughter, who is now a very happy little first grader. Being back with her mommy means more to her than anything in this world. The woman sees her youngest son regularly and hopes to regain custody of both of her sons.

A Brighter Day:
How Parents Can Help African American Youth

Why I Wrote This Book

The conversations that I had with this young mother had a profound effect on me, for they contain important messages about parenting, the unsteady place of children in society, and how bad choices can have generational outcomes. One of the messages that became clear to me from our conversations is that "When children aren't protected from danger, they're doomed or 'groomed' for failure." In fact, when the woman's daughter was only four years old, at least two people predicted that the child would be working the streets as a prostitute by the time she was 14 or that she'd have a baby of her own by then. Given how patterns can become generational, it is very likely that these negative predictions may come true.

I decided to write this book for a child's sake—for this little African American girl—and other African American children, because too many "bright lights" are being destroyed or set on a negative course early in life. Often, this path of failure starts in the home when we parents make choices that ultimately become harmful to our children. There are lots of reasons why some of us make such poor choices, including the following:

- We may have had poor parental role models ourselves.
- We may have become parents when we were children and never developed good parenting skills.
- We may put our own needs before those of our children.
- We may fail to see the long-term consequences of our actions.

Much has been written about the plight of Black children in America, and some of the statistics are indeed alarming.

Introduction

- Black children ages 1 to 16 are more likely to die during childhood than all other groups of children.[4]
- Black adolescents ages 12 to 17 years old are 20 times more likely than Whites in the same age group to be victims of serious violent crimes.
- Black children are also more likely than all other groups of children to be living below the poverty level,[5] to have a mother who gave birth when she was a child or an adolescent,[6] to not have a father in the home,[7] and to be living with a grandparent or other relative(s).[8]

This book contains stories, advice, and research that I have compiled primarily for African American parents who want to help their children have the best life they can have. I have met many of these parents during my travels and workshop presentations, and several have contacted me after hearing me on the radio or seeing me on television. But the book is also for teachers, social workers, therapists, counselors, mentors, and any other group that deals with African American children, parents, or guardians.

Children are naturally resilient—able to bounce back or recover from difficult circumstances. Bonnie Benard, one of the nation's leading experts on resiliency, found that even under the worst conditions most children turn out well as adults. But those who turn out well more than likely had at least one caring adult or "turnaround person" in their lives.[9] Ideally, parents should be the main positive role models in children's lives, but anyone can become a turnaround person— one who makes a positive impact on the life and development of a child from a challenging background. Anyone can help a child to become more resilient—able to bounce back and move in a positive direction.

A Brighter Day:
How Parents Can Help African American Youth

Parents and other adults can use the practical advice in this book to teach African American children how to navigate the storms of life so that they can have a brighter future. I'm especially hoping that this book will benefit Black mothers, single parents, parents enrolled in court-ordered parenting classes, and teens enrolled in parenting classes, for every single African American child deserves to have a great future.

Chapter 1

I Brought You into This World but *You* Might Take *Me* Out: What We Need to Know About Discipline

When I was a little girl, a friend of mine told me that her mother often said to her, "I brought you into this world, and I will take you out!" Whenever she appeared to be getting out of line, her mother said this to remind her who was boss. As we were growing up, many of us heard the same thing or something similar. In most cases, our parents or guardians meant no harm. What they wanted was for us to remember that we needed to treat our parents respectfully and to remember how to behave properly. Today, however, some parents who use this threat may be harming their children even though they may have good intentions. Others may not even pretend to have good intentions; they just engage in one harmful practice after another. One result is child abuse, which is common not only in the U.S. but throughout the world.[1] As I mentioned in the Introduction, Black children are more likely to die during childhood and to be subjected to violence than any other group of children.

One of the main reasons why child abuse is common is that most of us—including White, Latino, and Asian American parents—have never taken a parenting class. A female can have a baby, but that doesn't mean that she has a clue about how to take care of that baby. When a baby is born, we parents have the option of raising our children in the same manner in which our parents reared us or trying a totally different approach. Children are often abused by parents who follow a

1

cycle of generational abuse. These parents do what was done to them. If their mother or father beat them with an extension cord and they "turned out okay," they may adopt the same practice with their own children. If their mother or father called them the N word, they may call their children the same. Many adults don't understand the difference between abuse and discipline, so in the following sections I will explain the typical categories of abuse, the characteristics of perpetrators, the long-term consequences of child abuse, and what experts say about spanking and other forms of discipline. I will also describe several famous African Americans who overcame child abuse as well as prevention and intervention strategies. I conclude with the law of "sowing and reaping," a warning to parents about how child abuse can come back to haunt them.

Categories of Child Abuse

Contrary to popular opinion, child abuse doesn't just involve physically harming or sexually abusing a child. Any type of mistreatment can be considered child abuse. Child abuse categories typically include neglect, physical abuse, sexual abuse, and psychological maltreatment."[2]

Neglect. According to the Centers for Disease Control (CDC), neglect is the most common type of child abuse.[3] There are three types of neglect: emotional neglect, physical neglect, and educational neglect. Emotional neglect occurs when parents fail to make children "feel special, loved" and the family fails to be "a source of strength, support, and protection."[4] Children who are emotionally neglected may not gain weight, crave affection, and steal food.[5] Parents who subject children to emotional neglect may appear to be indifferent to the child, and they may seem to be depressed and/or they may behave in a bizarre manner. Parents who abuse drugs or alcohol may also be guilty of emotionally neglecting their children.[6]

Physical neglect occurs when parents don't provide children with enough food, water, and clean and decent clothing, and they don't take care of children's medical needs.[7] Physically neglected children may miss school frequently, beg or steal money, have a bad body odor, appear to be unclean, and need glasses and dental work.[8]

Parents who commit educational neglect fail to ensure that their children come to school on time and attend school regularly. They may appear to be unconcerned about whether or not their children complete their schoolwork. Later in this book, I'll describe specific ways in which African American parents can assist their children academically.

Emotional Abuse. Cursing at and insulting children are two common ways that parents can inflict emotional abuse on a child.[9] But it's more than this. According to the CDC, "Emotional abuse is any pattern of behavior that harms a child's emotional development or sense of self-worth. It includes frequent belittling, rejection threats, and the withholding of love and support."[10] Emotionally abused children may develop speech disorders, nervous disorders, and eating disorders. They may also become bedwetters, appear to enjoy hurting other children, be developmentally delayed, and behave in extreme ways.[11]

Physical Abuse. Physical abuse, the second most common type of abuse,[12] results in "physical injury due to punching, beating, kicking, biting, burning, shaking, or otherwise harming a child. Even if the parent or caretaker did not intend to harm the child, such acts are considered abuse when done purposefully."[13] Physically abused children may have bruises

3

on their bodies, and they may appear to be depressed, aggressive, or withdrawn. They may appear to be fearful of their parent(s) or caretaker(s). They may display anti-social behavior and become substance abusers.[14]

Sexual Abuse. Sexual abuse, which can be perpetrated by adults or other children, consists of touching or fondling a child "in a sexual way," forcing a child to touch the perpetrator's "body in a sexual way, and/or attempted [or actual] oral, anal, or vaginal intercourse" with a child.[15] Children who have been sexually abused may complain of having pain in the genitals, have frequent urinary tract or yeast infections, frequent sore throats, and genital or anal bleeding and discharges. They may become pregnant and/or contract sexually transmitted diseases. These children may have trouble sleeping, walking, or sitting, may avoid undressing in front of others, may wear extra layers of clothing, may act out sexually, or may develop problems at school.[16]

Perpetrators: Characteristics of Child Abusers

It seems to me that not a day passes without newspaper, television, and radio news reports carrying stories about horrible things that adults do to children. In recent years, we've been bombarded with stories about priests who sexually abuse children. In fact, as I was working on this chapter, *Deliver Us From Evil* was released. This documentary featured Oliver O'Grady, a former priest, who has admitted to sexually abusing "at least 25 children."[17] During the same month, a church pastor was arrested for molesting a little girl for seven years while she attended a Baptist School in Thousand Oaks, California.[18]

Of course, priests and pastors aren't the only child sexual predators. Just 10 days after the arrest of the former Thousand

4

Chapter 1: *I* Brought *You* into This World but *You* Might Take *Me* Out: What We Need to Know About Discipline

Oaks pastor, a San Diego male nurse received a 14-year prison sentence for "molesting a comatose toddler, who suffers from a rare condition and is unable to communicate."[19] Several months earlier, another male nurse at the same children's hospital was arrested for allegedly molesting "five young patients, all of whom were unable to communicate because of brain damage or other severe conditions."[20]

Although child abusers can work in any profession and come from any racial or ethnic background, any income bracket, and be either male or female, the ones that tend to shock us the most are parents who abuse. Foster parents are supposed to be *care*takers who have opened their homes and taken related classes in order to help children who have been abused or neglected. Yet numerous foster parents have been arrested for abusing the very children they were being paid to help. In 2003, Americans were shocked to learn that Raymond and Vanessa Jackson, a highly respected, church-attending African American couple in New Jersey with several adopted children, had been arrested for aggravated assault and starving four of their children. The oldest boy, a teenager, only weighed 45 pounds when his parents were arrested. Neighbors had caught him "rummaging through their trash."[21] In 2004, another foster parent, David Schaper, a church youth pastor, was arrested in Oregon and charged with raping three girls ranging from two to nine years old. Schaper's wife ran a daycare center out of their home, and she allowed him to take care of the children when she was away from home.[22] In 2006, Melanie Ochs, a Las Vegas foster mother, was arrested for child abuse after she murdered a seven-month-old baby. The child "died from blunt force trauma to the head." He had been living with Ochs since he was three days old.[23]

Even though we hear horrible stories about abusive foster parents and adoptive parents, in reality, foster parents, legal guardians, and unmarried partners of parents are a lot less likely to abuse children than are biological parents and stepparents. In fact, "nonparent perpetrators" account for only about 10 percent of the total percentage of child abusers. On the other hand, "nearly 84 percent of victims [are] abused by a parent acting alone or with another person," and mothers are more likely than all other groups to be guilty of inflicting abuse on a child.[24]

The media report so many cases of parents abusing children that the public may have become immune. But in my case, this hasn't happened, and I continue to be shocked each time a new case surfaces. In 2005, for instance, I was horrified when a couple in Utah was arrested for torturing, starving, and pulling out the toenails of several of their children.[25]

During that same year, the Precious Doe case, a mystery that had received widespread media coverage, was solved. In 2001, the headless body of this three-year-old Black child was found in Kansas City, Missouri, yet no one came forward to claim the body. Because her identity was unknown, she was nicknamed "Precious Doe." This case confused authorities for years. However, one man, Alonzo Washington, a community activist and child advocate, wouldn't let the public or authorities forget about this child. In 2005, thanks to the persistence of Washington who didn't "want people 'to forget there was a child discarded like trash,'" there was a break in the case. In the end, the mother and stepfather of the child (whose real name was Erica Michelle Maria Green) were arrested. The stepfather had kicked the child in the head, and he and her mother had allowed her to suffer without medical attention for about two days before she finally died.[26]

Chapter 1: *I* Brought *You* into This World but *You* Might Take *Me* Out: What We Need to Know About Discipline

Researchers have drawn some interesting conclusions about child abusers and the types of parents and caregivers who are most likely to abuse. One of the most surprising findings is that "Over 90% of abusive parents do not have a psychotic or criminal personality."[27] Researchers have identified the following list of parents as being high risk for child abuse:

1. Single parents who have few, if any, friends to help them with child care, who are lonely, who had an unplanned pregnancy, who don't know much about child development or appropriate child behavior, and who are substance abusers are considered to be high-risk parents.[28]

2. Parents who live in poverty, in communities where there is lots of violence, who experience lots of stressful events, and who were teenage parents are high risk.[29]

3. Parents who have experienced spousal abuse, have a limited education, and have a mental disability are high risk.[30]

4. Parents who have so-called "high-risk children," infants who were born prematurely, are mentally retarded, have ongoing medical problems, or are colicky babies are high risk.[31]

One of the most well-known characteristics of parents who are most likely to abuse is that many of them come from abusive childhoods. It's hard to pinpoint the actual numbers because they vary depending on who is reporting them. For example, according to one report, "10-40% of abusive parents have experienced physical abuse as children."[32] A report from the American Academy of Family Physicians states, "Parents who were abused as children are more likely than other parents to abuse their own children.[33] According to a third report, not only were most abusive parents abused or neglected during childhood, but "many abusers view themselves as victims in life generally or in the parent-child relationship in particular. They feel they have lost control of their children and their own lives."[34] In other words, child abuse can become a generational cycle. It can also lead to many other problems, including the ones I mentioned above under each subcategory of child abuse.

Long-Term Consequences

One of the saddest aspects of child abuse is that it has been linked to many long-term consequences. CDC researchers who conducted the Adverse Childhood Experiences Study found that children who had been abused, neglected, or exposed to "other traumatic stressors" were more likely than others to experience the following problems and indulge in the following behaviors as adults:

- have unplanned pregnancies
- attempt suicide
- contract sexually transmitted diseases
- have multiple sexual partners
- develop heart disease, liver disease, and/or pulmonary disease
- use illegal drugs and/or abuse alcohol
- have a child die
- experience depression
- become involved in an abusive relationship with a partner.[35]

Child abuse can also affect people who are not directly or indirectly connected to the original abuser. The interviews that Helen Morrison, a forensic psychiatrist, has conducted with serial killers illustrate this point. Even though Morrison believes that serial killers become this way as a result of a genetic problem, not child abuse, many of her interview subjects were abused as children. One of these serial murderers, Richard Macek, admitted that his father was physically abusive."[36] When he committed suicide in prison, Macek was serving a life sentence for murder. John Wayne Gacy, one of the most notorious serial killers that Morrison interviewed, had a father who not only hated his son but verbally and physically abused his wife and children as well. Gacy, who liked to dress up as a clown, eventually was convicted of killing 33 people and executed by lethal injection.[37] Bobby Joe Long, who was sentenced to death for killing numerous women, grew up hating both of his parents, especially his mother, a single parent.[38]

Like Morrison, Anna Salter, a psychologist, has interviewed individuals who have done horrible things to others. Salter has interviewed rapists, sadists, psychopaths, and other types of sexual predators, including those who prey exclusively on children. Salter doesn't necessarily believe that most sexual predators who prey on children were abused themselves, but she has found that often children who are sexually abused had previously been neglected by their parents, had a single mother, and/or didn't have a close relationship with their fathers. This made them easy targets for child sexual predators.[39]

Some of the most interesting, but also chilling, work that shows the long-term effects of child abuse deals with sociopathy. Sociopaths have been described as people who don't have a conscience and are unable to empathize with others. Martha Stout, a clinical psychologist who worked at the Harvard Medical School for 25 years, refers to sociopaths as "ice people," "cold blooded" individuals who use charm, manipulation, and deception to take advantage of others. Even though they account for less than five percent of the total U.S. population, they cause a great deal of harm to society. The three main theories about sociopathy are that genetics, environment, and the way that sociopaths process emotional stimuli may all be contributing factors. Culture and the way children are reared may also play a role in determining which individuals become sociopaths.[40] Ken Magid and Carole A. McKelvey, the authors of *High Risk: Children Without a Conscience*, believe that abuse and a child's failure to bond or attach to the primary caregiver during the first year of life can cause children to grow up to become sociopaths.[41]

Although some researchers believe that it's impossible to determine if a person is a sociopath before age 18, others have found that some common signs of sociopathy often surface during childhood. These signs include being cruel to other children and animals, being fascinated with blood and gore, self-destructiveness, hoarding and stealing food and other items, excessive lying, phoniness, poor eye contact, and speech and learning problems.[42]

A famous case of a child who displayed sociopathic tendencies at an early age is that of Mary Bell. Mary, who lived in England, came from an extremely abusive background. Not only was her mother a prostitute, but she reportedly made Mary have sex with men and gave her drugs. When she was only 11 years old, Mary was convicted of murdering two little boys. Her coldness, ruthlessness, lack of emotion, and other behaviors convinced some experts that she was indeed a sociopath.[43]

Several experts were also convinced that 11-year-old Robert "Yummy" Sandifer, an African American Chicago gang member, was a sociopath. Like Mary Bell, Sandifer had come from an abusive background. According to a *Time* magazine article, his mother was a teenage-drug addict when she gave birth to him, and "as a baby, he was burned and beaten." He lived in lots of different places, joined a gang, and was repeatedly arrested. In 1994, Sandifer's own gang killed him after he murdered a 14-year-old girl. Some of his neighbors were actually relieved when he died because he had developed such a bad reputation. A 13-year-old who knew him said, "Nobody didn't like that boy. Nobody gonna miss him."[44] Some commentators said that the horrible abuse and bad parenting that Sandifer had experienced had caused him to become a sociopath. Others sympathized with the little 11-year-old boy whose short life had been so tragic.

Despite the fact that there is still controversy over whether or not child abuse leads to sociopathy and even serial killing, the link between child abuse and prison incarceration rates is much clearer. The Children's Defense Fund found that "Children in the juvenile justice system are more likely to have a history of child abuse and neglect than children outside the system."[45] Statistics from Childhelp indicate that nearly 40 percent of women in prison and 14 percent of men in prison were victims of child abuse.[46] An ACLU report revealed an even stronger link between prison incarceration and an abusive background. According to "Words from Prison—Did You Know. . .?":

- "79% of women in federal and state prisons reported physical abuse and over 60% reported past sexual abuse."
- "Women in prison are three to four times more likely than male prisoners to have experienced abuse, whether as a child or adult."
- "An estimated 56% of those women in prison who have experienced abuse report that their abuse

included rape, and another 13% reported an attempted rape."

- "54% of girls incarcerated in U.S. juvenile correctional settings have been sexually abused, 61% have been physically abused, and the majority of those girls have been abused multiple times."
- "Over 80% of girls in juvenile detention had run away from home and over half had attempted suicide."
- "Two-thirds of women in prison in the United States are women of color."
- "In 2004, Black women were 4.5 times more likely than White women to be incarcerated."
- "African American women's incarceration rates for all crimes increased by 800% since 1986, compared to an increase of 400% for women of all races."
- "Girls of color who are victims of abuse are more likely to be processed by the criminal justice system and labeled as offenders than White girls. White girls who are abused have a better chance of being treated as victims and referred to child welfare and mental health systems."[47]

From a Background of Shame to the Hall of Fame: Victors and Resilient Survivors of Child Abuse

Obviously, child abuse can lead to numerous problems in adulthood. Many adults, such as serial killer and rapist Ted Bundy, cult-leader Charles Manson, and serial rapist and murderer Kenneth Bianchi, were abused as children.[48] Even though some child abuse victims turn out badly, most child abuse victims do not. For every story about a child abuse victim who remained a victim and even went on to victimize others, there are lots of stories about victims who became victors. In fact, many extremely successful African Americans fit this description.

For example, one of my favorite gospel singers, Donny McClurkin, was raped repeatedly by two relatives during childhood, and he experienced several other hardships. However, McClurkin made a decision to use music as an outlet for his pain.[49] His songs "Stand" ("After you've done all you can, you just stand and endure...") and "We Fall Down, but We Get Up" have uplifted me on many dark days.

Tavis Smiley, one of the most famous Black journalists in the U.S., is another great example. Smiley, who was selected as "one of America's 50 most promising young leaders,"[50] was beaten so badly by his father during childhood that he had to be hospitalized. Afterwards, he and his sister, who was also beaten, were placed in different foster homes. Instead of letting his difficult childhood ruin his life, Smiley chose to become victorious. Today, he is a prolific author and a popular television show host.[51]

Tyler Perry, an extremely gifted African American author, playwright, director, actor, comedian, and producer, is another example of an individual who refused to let an abusive childhood ruin his future. When he was growing up in New Orleans, Perry often saw his father physically and verbally abusing his mother. His father also abused his son even when he was a teenager. Once, when he was 17 years old, his father threw him to the floor and stomped him. Things got so bad at times that Perry had "dark thoughts of killing his father—or himself—just to get some relief."[52] Instead of letting his pain compel him to murder his father or destroy himself, Perry channeled it into writing. Today, as a result of his hilarious, entertaining, and informative plays and movies, including

A Brighter Day:
How Parents Can Help African American Youth

Diary of a Mad Black Woman, *Madea's Family Reunion*, and *Madea Goes to Jail*, Perry is one of the wealthiest and most successful individuals in America.

Most people who are familiar with Quincy Jones's long and productive career in the music industry would probably agree that this man is a genius. He won an Emmy award, Ebony Music awards, NAACP awards, and humanitarian awards. He won Grammy Awards for Producer of the Year, Album of the Year, and Record of the Year, and has been nominated for numerous other Grammys. In 1986, Jones won an American Music Award for "We are the World," a song that brought attention to and raised money for poor people in Africa. He has won awards from MTV and has been nominated for awards from the Academy of Motion Pictures, the Golden Globes, and the Academy of Television Arts and Sciences. Jones has also received nearly 30 honorary doctorates and academic awards.

But it's Jones's music that the public knows best. He arranged the music for the movie *The Color Purple* and theme songs for several television shows, including *Sanford and Son* and *The Cosby Show*. Jones also produced Michael Jackson's *Thriller*, which became "the bestselling album of all time."[53]

Even though Jones is successful today, his road to success was difficult. During childhood, he experienced many stressful situations. For example, he was so poor that he had to eat rats! One of the most challenging circumstances was his mother's ongoing mental illness that caused her to eventually be institutionalized. After one frightening visit with his mother, Jones became fearful that she would escape from the mental institution and kill him. Later, his father married a woman who fed her own children well but mistreated Quincy and his brother. But when he was 11 years old, Quincy finally found a way to cope with all of the pain inside of himself; music brought him peace in a way that nothing else did. Since then, he has created songs that have brought peace and joy to countless people.[54]

Like Quincy Jones, Antwone Fisher also used music to deal with the many problems he experienced during childhood and adolescence. Fisher, the son of a teenager who gave birth to him in a juvenile detention facility, was placed in foster care as a baby. Although his first foster mother loved him and treated him well, the second foster mother and her husband made his life a "living hell."[55] During the many years Fisher lived with the Pickett family, he was beaten, verbally abused, and sexually assaulted. One of the saddest aspects of the abuse is that Mr. and Mrs. Pickett were extremely religious people, yet they repeatedly mistreated a child whom they were being paid to raise. One of the ways that Fisher coped was by listening to music. This made him feel safe. Although the odds were against him, Fisher became successful. After joining the Navy and getting help for his dyslexia, he wrote his best selling autobiography, *Finding Fish: A Memoir*. This book was made into a great movie in which Denzel Washington starred.[56]

One of the best-known examples of an African American who became successful after being abused as a child is television talk show host Oprah Winfrey. During childhood, Winfrey experienced poverty, physical abuse, verbal abuse, and sexual abuse. On one of her television shows that aired in late 2006, she spoke about becoming pregnant as a teenager, hiding the pregnancy, and mourning her baby's short life. Whereas Jones and Fisher found peace through music, Winfrey read books that helped her deal with her difficult childhood.[57] Instead of becoming another negative Black

A Brighter Day:
How Parents Can Help African American Youth

statistic, Oprah has become one of the most famous and wealthiest women in the world. *Time* magazine called her one of "the most important people of the century."[58] Like Quincy Jones, Winfrey has received numerous awards and honors, and she has tried to improve social conditions through her work. She has worked hard to expose the effects of child abuse, and to motivate the public to help law enforcement agencies track down child sexual predators. In addition to producing and acting in movies and owning her own production company, Winfrey has donated huge sums of money to build a girls' school in South Africa, purchased homes for needy families, and assisted other struggling individuals.

Winfrey's mentor, Maya Angelou, is another famous African American who overcame many problems, including child abuse. When she was seven, Angelou was raped by her mother's boyfriend. "When she later heard the news that an uncle had killed her attacker, she felt that her words had killed the man. She fell silent and did not speak for five years."[59] During those silent years, she read poetry and memorized poems and sonnets. At age nine, she began writing her thoughts in a journal.[60] Angelou eventually began to speak again, and today, people throughout the world have heard her "voice," mostly through her writing. In addition to publishing many books, especially her famous autobiographical series beginning with *I Know Why the Caged Bird Sings*, she has composed songs, appeared on numerous television programs, won many awards and honors, and read her poem, "On the Pulse of the Morning," at President Bill Clinton's 1993 inauguration.[61] One of the main themes of her work is, "People can overcome the obstacles they face. 'We may encounter many defeats, but we must not be defeated... We are much stronger than we appear to be, and may be much better than we allow ourselves to be.'"[62]

Tavis Smiley, Donnie McClurkin, Oprah Winfrey, Maya Angelou, Quincy Jones, Tyler Perry, and Antwone Fisher are just a few examples of famous African Americans who overcame childhood abuse. Although most child abuse victims won't ever become as famous as these individuals, many will become parents or are parents already. Because child abuse often creates a generational cycle in which the victim grows up to victimize others, I want to devote the next section to suggesting some appropriate discipline strategies for those of us who may have been abuse victims ourselves and for other parents and caregivers of Black children. I will focus on four groups of children: babies, toddlers, elementary school students, and preteens and teenagers. But first, let me discuss spanking, a very controversial topic.

To Spank or Not to Spank

There are two viewpoints regarding spanking. Some people believe that any form of physical punishment is wrong, and others believe that spanking, as long as it doesn't become abusive, is appropriate at times. In fact, many who are in favor of spanking, especially some Black people I know, quote Proverbs 13:24, which says, "He that spareth his rod hateth his son: but he that loveth him chasteneth him betimes." They believe this biblical scripture supports their view that spanking is sometimes necessary.

I have always believed that spanking, as long as it is *spanking* and not abuse, is necessary at times. When my own three children were growing up, both my husband and I spanked them when we believed their behavior warranted it.

A Brighter Day:
How Parents Can Help African American Youth

In my case, I would usually tell the child how many swats he or she was going to get beforehand. I usually used a ruler and sometimes I used a small belt. Telling the child that he or she was going to get three swats or five swats meant that the discipline was structured, I wasn't out of control, and the child knew what to expect. But a lot of people, including some African American experts, disagree with my position.

In *Raising Black Children: Two Leading Psychiatrists Confront the Educational, Social and Emotional Problems Facing Black Children,* Dr. James P. Comer (for whom I have tremendous respect) and Dr. Alvin F. Poussaint, famous African American experts, discuss spanking and other topics related to childrearing. According to the authors, there is evidence that many children who are spanked grow up to be healthy and successful individuals. However, they believe that there are more effective ways to discipline a child than spanking. Some of the strategies these doctors recommend include:

- talking to children about their misbehavior
- requiring children to accept responsibility for their actions
- explaining to children why you are displeased with their behavior
- talking to children about your expectations of appropriate behavior.

These experts are mostly concerned about the possibility of parents losing control and using their own frustration as an excuse to spank children.[63]

Another expert, Michael Connor, an African American Professor Emeritus at California State University, Long Beach, is strongly opposed to spanking under any circumstance. In November 2006, my husband and I heard Dr. Connor give a

Chapter 1: *I* Brought *You* into This World but *You* Might Take *Me* Out: What We Need to Know About Discipline

keynote address at a luncheon sponsored by The Association of Pan-African Doctoral Scholars, Inc. According to Connor, parents use spanking as an excuse to alleviate their own tension, and children get spanked merely for "acting like kids." When adults resort to spanking, Connor said, they are acting immaturely. "Why you wanna hit somebody for acting their age?" he asked. "Why don't *you* act your age?" Throughout his speech, he emphasized that, "We need to give up corporal punishment. It does not work... Hitting somebody to solve a problem does not solve a problem."

Regardless of what the experts say, spanking has long been used among African Americans, and undoubtedly it will continue to be passed on from one generation to another within many families. My goal in this section is not to convince parents to give up spanking. Since I've already admitted that I spanked my own children when they were growing up, I'd be a hypocrite if I told other parents not to do so. My goal, however, is to convince those of you who do believe that spanking is an appropriate form of discipline to exercise wisdom, caution, restraint, and good sense when you do so. Extension cords, belt buckles, telephone cords, frying pans, and anything else besides a ruler, switch, or small belt should never be used, in my opinion. Furthermore, parents should never spank when they're angry or use the fact that they've had a bad day as an excuse to spank a child. Parents should never leave bruises or welts on children, and as I emphasize in the next section on parenting strategies recommended by experts, infants and babies should *never ever* be spanked.

Babies
When I was a little girl who was actively involved in a small Pentecostal church in Otay, California, I once heard a

A Brighter Day:
How Parents Can Help African American Youth

story that sent chills down my spine. One night, during Testimony Service, a time when anyone could get up and testify about God's grace, life's trials, or deliverance from a problem, the eldest woman in the church stood up. Instead of testifying, it turned out that this frail old lady wanted to give parents some advice. She began by saying that too many children were out of control because their parents weren't bringing them up properly. Although I don't remember the exact words she used to criticize bad parents, I'll never forget what she said before she sat down: "I started spanking all of my children when they were nine days old."

I was still in elementary school at the time and a victim of child abuse myself, yet I knew something was terribly wrong with hitting a nine-day-old baby. Her words disturbed me so much that when I got home, I told my mother what the little old lady had said. "Nine days old!" my mother exclaimed. "I waited until ya'll were three months old before I started spanking you!" For the second time that night my mind began to whirl out of control. I thought of newborn babies at nine days old and three-month-old babies being hit, and even though two adults whom I respected had said it was okay to spank them, I disagreed. But I kept my thoughts to myself, for opening my mouth could have led to a brutal beating.

Although the old woman's words and my mother's comments shocked me, research has shown that babies are very likely to be abused by parents. In fact, in recent years, a new term, "shaken-baby syndrome," has been created to describe the common practice of shaking a crying baby to silence the infant. Some babies have even been shaken to death. According to Dr. Lesa Bethea of the American Academy of Family Physicians, of the nearly 200,000 children who "suffer severe or life-threatening" injuries each year, "1,000

Chapter 1: *I* Brought *You* into This World but *You* Might Take *Me* Out: What We Need to Know About Discipline

to 2,000 children die as a result of abuse. Of these deaths, 80 percent involve children younger than five years of age, and 40 percent involve children younger than one year of age."[64]

Just as talking is one of the main ways that older children and adults communicate, crying is the way that a baby communicates. Babies cry to say they're hungry, in need of a diaper change, need to be held, and are scared. Unfortunately, adults with poor parenting skills who don't understand child development or who were victims of child abuse themselves may misunderstand the reasons why babies cry. I've heard some older African American women, for example, claim that babies cry because they're "spoiled." These women believe that the best way to deal with crying babies is to put them in a room alone and let them cry until they learn—the hard way—to stop being so "spoiled."

Babies are actually a fascinating group of individuals to study, and what happens to children during the first year of life can set the stage for the rest of their lives. As Magid and McKelvey state in *High Risk: Children Without a Conscience*, babies who don't bond with their primary caregivers grow up to exhibit sociopathic tendencies. Mothers and other primary caregivers who don't hold, stroke, talk to, make proper eye contact, smile, play with, and take care of the baby's other needs can cause infants to become "unattached, character-disturbed" children.[65] Erik Erikson, one of the most famous child development experts in history, described eight stages of development. According to Erikson, babies need to believe their mothers or other main caregivers are reliable, consistent, predictable, and confident about their parenting abilities. Based on how they are treated by their primary caregivers, babies either learn to trust or mistrust these individuals.[66]

During my years as a Peace Corps Volunteer in Africa in the early 1980s, I made some interesting observations about the differences between how many babies are reared in the U.S. versus in Africa. In Africa, I saw low-income and rural mothers keep their babies strapped to their backs throughout the entire day. When these women went to the market, they took their babies with them. When they cooked food, their babies were right on their backs. When these women chatted with neighbors, served meals, cleaned their houses, or did anything, their babies were there. Whenever a baby would cry, instead of assuming the baby was merely spoiled and needed to be taught a lesson, the mother would take the baby off of her back and nurse the child. In other words, the African mothers made their babies and their needs a top priority.

The CDC developed "Positive Parenting Tips for Healthy Child Development" for the parents of babies, toddlers, and older children. According to the CDC, from ages zero to one year old, babies need parents to do the following:

- Talk to them so they can learn language and be soothed by the parent's voice.
- Read to them.
- Sing to them.
- Play music for them to help them develop an appreciation for music and math skills.
- Praise them.
- Give them lots of loving attention.
- Cuddle and hold them to help them feel safe.[67]

Like the African mothers I observed, parents who meet their babies' physical and emotional needs during the first year of life create a foundation that can have long-term benefits. As the CDC reported, "The way you cuddle, hold, and play with your baby will set the basis for how he will interact with you and others."[68]

Chapter 1: *I* Brought *You* into This World but *You* Might Take *Me* Out: What We Need to Know About Discipline

Toddlers

In November 2005, I was napping on an airplane that was headed for Baltimore when a commotion woke me up. No, it wasn't a terrorist attack, nor was it engine trouble. The brouhaha was caused by an unruly toddler in the row in front of me. He was yelling his head off and punching the woman (perhaps his frazzled mother) who was holding him. During the four-hour flight, the child scratched her, knocked her glasses off several times, and repeatedly pulled her headphones off. He made it clear that he wasn't going to let her watch the in-flight movie. Each time that the woman and teenager sitting next to her tried to calm the child, the same pattern occurred: he'd be quiet for a few minutes and then start acting out again. I kept wondering why he wouldn't stop crying. Did he have an earache? After all, many travelers develop ear problems while airborne. However, the longer I watched the intensity of his attacks on the woman, the more I began to suspect that this toddler was used to having his way. He obviously didn't fear any consequences about clawing the woman's face and neck and repeatedly knocking off her glasses or pulling off her headphones.

I felt somewhat sorry for the woman and teenager because they appeared to be helpless. But I also felt sorry for the toddler because his ears might have been hurting. They couldn't fix the situation, and they knew lots of people on the plane were glaring at them and grumbling about the toddler's shrieks. But, I was also angry. After all, I couldn't sleep or relax because each time that I dozed off, the child's tantrums would jolt me awake. I'm sure everyone just wanted the mother to shut the kid up. In fact, I actually saw several people stand up and give the mother dirty looks.

A Brighter Day:
How Parents Can Help African American Youth

This recurring scene reminded me of a similar incident I'd witnessed a few months earlier when I was flying home from a speaking engagement. After the passengers had gotten on the plane, we learned that we wouldn't be able to leave the ground. Again, it wasn't a terrorist attack, nor was it engine trouble. Once again, the problem centered around a mother and a small child. In this case, a screaming little boy threw a fit and refused to let his mother strap him into his assigned seat. Either he couldn't understand or he didn't care that once the plane took off and the "fasten your seat-belt" sign went off, he could climb back on his mommy's lap for most of the remainder of the flight. Each time that the mother tried to place him in his seat as the flight attendant had insisted, the boy screamed, swung his arms wildly, and stiffened his body, making it impossible for his mother to force him into his seat and strap him in.

Once other passengers began to realize what was delaying our departure, many became visibly and vocally angry. Someone yelled, "Beat the kid!" Someone else yelled, "No, beat the mother! It's not the kid's fault she can't control him." At least two passengers began to argue about who was actually at fault. Although I was just as annoyed as everyone else, I kept my mouth shut and felt somewhat sorry for the mother. I knew she was embarrassed and felt helpless.

Both of these stories involved young children whose level of comprehension was quite limited. Nevertheless, the stories contain an important message for parents and primary caregivers. The lesson is, "If you raise a 'Bebe's Kid,' he'll shame you one day." Bebe's Kid refers to an animated movie that was popular many years ago about a Black woman, Bebe, and her unruly kids. These kids were incorrigible, and they had a bad reputation throughout the neighborhood. Since then,

Chapter 1: *I* Brought *You* into This World but *You* Might Take *Me* Out: What We Need to Know About Discipline

the term "Bebe's Kids" has become popular in the Black community and refers to undisciplined children. The Bebe's Kids' syndrome often starts when children are toddlers.

Toddlers—children who are two or three years old—are a very unique group of individuals. They want to be independent, and they want to have their own way. Because many toddlers are strong-willed, this age group poses special challenges for parents. According to the CDC, "Because of [the] child's growing desire to assert her independence, this stage is often called the 'terrible twos.' However, this can be an exciting time for you and your toddler. He will experience huge intellectual, social, and emotional changes that will help him to explore his new world, and make sense of it."[69] The CDC recommends that parents of toddlers do the following:

- have a regular time to read to the toddler
- play games with the toddler
- teach the toddler children's songs
- take walks with the toddler.[70]

Drs. Comer and Poussaint also urge parents to talk to toddlers in a firm but not angry tone. Parents should be fair, reasonable, and not overprotective, and they should never ridicule children.[71]

Preschoolers

Preschoolers are three to five years old. Like toddlers, they want to become more independent from their parents. They are interested in children and adults outside of their own families, and they like to explore their surroundings.[72]

Preschoolers are known for displaying aggressiveness and temper tantrums. Comer and Poussaint recommend that parents help preschoolers deal with their frustrations and

A Brighter Day:
How Parents Can Help African American Youth

disappointments through healthy discipline practices, such as giving children time outs (sending them to another room to cool off) and talking to them calmly about expectations of behavior.[73] According to the CDC, parents should also:

- continue to read to preschoolers
- take them to libraries and bookstores
- encourage them to play with other children in order "to learn the value of sharing and friendship"
- help them develop good language skills by using complete sentences when speaking to preschoolers and by teaching them "to use the correct words and phrases"
- "be clear and consistent when disciplining" preschoolers, and "model the behavior that [parents] expect from [them]."[74]

Elementary Students

The elementary school years constitute an important period for children and parents. Not only do children become more independent during this time, but their attitudes about school and their peers become stronger and can set the tone for the rest of their school years. According to Comer and Poussaint, from age's five to eight, several important changes occur in children. Children become more aware of racial differences, and they have a stronger desire to belong. During this period, parents must find appropriate ways to help children deal with racism and prejudice, learn how to get along with others, develop good manners, better understand the world around them, and help them to develop morally by talking about and modeling good behavior.[75] CDC experts recommend the following parenting tips for parents of 9–11 year olds:

- Spend time with your children.
- Talk to children about their friends, challenges they will face, and accomplishments.
- Attend school events, and get to know their teachers.
- Encourage them to participate in sports and other activities.
- Help them develop a sense of right and wrong.
- "Discuss peer pressure with children.
- "Help children to become more responsible by having them do chores and helping them learn how to spend money wisely.
- "Get to know the family members of your children's friends.
- "Teach them to treat others respectfully.
- "Talk to your child about what to expect during puberty.
- "Be consistent in enforcing rules.
- "Be affectionate and honest with [children] and do things together as a family."[76]

Pre-Teens and Teenagers

At the end of her first year of teaching during the late 1980s, one of my teacher education classmates exclaimed to me, "I hate teenagers, and I don't even want to see any movies with teenagers in them!" Needless to say, she'd had a very difficult school year, and that June, she decided to quit teaching completely. But long before I heard her make this statement, the aunt of one of my closest friends made a similar statement: "I hate teenagers!" she declared. At the time, she had two teenage sons. These women were merely stating what a lot of parents, teachers, social workers, and law enforcement

A Brighter Day:
How Parents Can Help African American Youth

personnel already know: The teenage years are difficult, not only for teenagers but also for individuals who come in contact with them. During this time, the desire for independence increases as does peer pressure. A once sweet, obedient son or daughter may begin to act defiantly, and parents and teenagers can become locked in a cycle of battles.

Because of the tremendous pressure on teens, these years can also be very dangerous, a time when youth may make decisions that can ruin their lives forever. Dr. Jawanza Kunjufu, an education and parenting expert, and the author of numerous books about African American children, said that by age 12, many Black children are ready to join gangs, start using illegal drugs, and they may even become sexually active at this time.[77] Young African American males 13 to 18 years old "control the community" and create fear in many individuals.[78] At this point, some parents who may have previously modeled good parenting practices may make crucial mistakes by giving their sons too much freedom. For example, as Kunjufu found, parents may try to become "buddies" with their children instead of the legitimate authority figure in the home, and they may permit their teens to make decisions that the parents should be making, such as whether or not to attend church, tutoring sessions, and certain extracurricular activities.[79] Kunjufu recommends the following tips specifically for parents of African American male teenagers:

- Find a support group to discuss problems and concerns with other parents.
- Become actively involved in your children's lives from infancy through age 18.
- Help teens recognize and develop their talents.

Chapter 1: *I* Brought *You* into This World but *You* Might Take *Me* Out: What We Need to Know About Discipline

- Expose teens to careers that are related to their talents.
- Help teens find nonviolent problem-solving solutions.
- Teach Black males how to become decent men.
- Consider enrolling Black males in rites of passage programs.
- Help teens improve their self-esteem and self-image.
- Help teens understand the importance of spiritually.[80]

Drs. Comer and Poussaint emphasize that from the time children reach nine years of age, *talking* should be parents' main type of discipline. They believe that from this point on, physical punishment becomes ineffective, and spankings can cause a child to physically retaliate against a parent. Comer and Poussaint recommend the following tips for parents of teens:

- Treat teens respectfully.
- Allow teens to become more independent as they become more responsible.
- Avoid giving commands.
- Become aware of negative behaviors that might be cries for help.
- Make peace whenever possible.
- Use praise for good behavior.
- Be actively involved in teens' lives and interested in their hobbies.
- Avoid spanking and yelling.
- Only withdraw privileges when talking and explanations have failed to produce the desired behavior.
- Keep in mind that the main goal of discipline should be to help youth develop into responsible, well-behaved individuals.[81]

A Brighter Day:
How Parents Can Help African American Youth

The Law of Sowing and Reaping

In his excellent autobiography, *What I Know for Sure*, radio and television talk show host Tavis Smiley described a brutal beating his father gave him and his sister Phyllis when Tavis was a seventh grader. After the pastor of their church wrongfully accused Tavis and Phyllis of misbehaving during Children's Church, when they arrived home, their father used an extension cord to teach them a lesson about how to behave. But, the father lost control and beat the children so badly that both ended up in the hospital. The lesson that the children learned wasn't the one their father intended. What they learned was to mistrust both their father, who lost control of his emotions and was driven by anger as he inflicted blow after blow, and their mother, who didn't stop him from abusing them. As he lay in the hospital recovering from his wounds, anger, hurt, and confusion consumed Tavis. After being released from the hospital, Phyllis was placed in a foster home with a White family. She never returned home, never recovered from the beating, and became an angry, and rebellious woman. Tavis was placed in a foster home with a Black minister and his wife but often thought of getting revenge on his parents who lived near his new home. Unlike his sister Phyllis and countless other abused children, Tavis eventually found healthy ways of dealing with his hatred of his parents and his desire to "get even with them." His love and respect for his family outweighed the negative feelings that surfaced from the beating, and he returned home after several months in foster care. Nevertheless, the beating changed him forever in both positive and negative ways.[82]

I entitled this chapter "*I* Brought You Into This World but *You* May Take *Me* Out" because some child abuse victims grow up to become adults who victimize the very parents who abused them. These children never get over their rage and need for revenge, and as a result, the parents reap what they've sowed. The children turn into adults who "return the favor" when the parents are too old and feeble to defend themselves. A good example is a story that my grandmother Francis told me more than 20 years ago.

When he was an old man, Francis's great grandfather hanged himself because he believed that his children were mean to him. At the time, all of his children, including the youngest—my great grandmother—were adults. Years later, during one of my trips to Texas, my grandmother showed me the tree from which he hanged himself. To date, no one has told me why *all* of my great great grandfather's adult children were mean to him. Therefore, I had to draw my own conclusions. What I suspect is that if *every single one* of his adult children treated him badly in old age, he must have been getting paid back for things he had done to them. "If not one of his children treated him kindly," I thought, "they must've learned to be mean from him." Since at least one of his children grew up to inflict brutal beatings on her own children and some of her grandchildren, and based on what I've heard from various relatives about the mean deeds of my great great grandfather's other offspring, this meanness could have been taught during childhood and may explain why his children treated him so badly when he was too old to defend himself.

A more recent story involves a woman who used to attend a church where I was once a member. This woman kept several foster children, and it was rumored that she wasn't very nice to them. She was extremely strict, critical, and some of her "discipline" practices seemed harsh and even abusive. When this woman grew old, she became ill and couldn't take care

A Brighter Day:
How Parents Can Help African American Youth

of herself. *Not one* of her adult children wanted to be bothered with her. Instead, they insisted she be placed in a nursing home. When I heard how her children were treating her, I felt very sorry for her. Then a friend of mine who also knew the woman and her family quite well reminded me of how the elderly woman had treated all those little foster children long ago. "Before it's over," my friend told me, "she has some more reaping to do."

By reaping, my friend meant payback, for like me, she believes in the law of retribution. In other words, we believe that the old saying, "What goes around comes back around," is true. If a farmer plants a healthy apple seed in fertile soil, that seed will become an apple tree, not a peach, plum, or orange tree. If parents plant good seeds in their children through healthy parenting practices and instilling good values in them, more than likely their children will turn out well in life. Of course, there are always exceptions, but in most cases children who grow up in loving, healthy, and supportive homes grow up to become decent adults.

The CDC's Adverse Childhood Experiences study concluded that children who experience abuse or neglect can develop many problems as adults, including medical and emotional problems. Many resort to harmful behaviors. Furthermore, as I mentioned previously, child abuse can launch a generational cycle in which abused children grow up to abuse their own children and even their elderly parents.

In fact, just as child abuse is a national problem affecting countless children, elder abuse is also a huge problem. According to the American Psychological Association:

> Every year, an estimated 2.1 million older Americans are victims of physical, psychological, or other forms of abuse and neglect. Those statistics may not tell the whole

story. For every case of elder abuse and neglect that is reported to authorities, experts estimate that there may be as many as five cases that have not been reported.[83]

Types of elder abuse include physical, sexual, emotional, neglect, verbal, and financial,[84] and the perpetrators are often family members. Although there are lots of other causes of elder abuse, a recurring message in the research is what I've already said in this chapter: Child abuse can create a generational cycle of violence. Most abused children don't grow up to abuse their parents, but some do. "Abusive parents can unknowingly teach children that abuse is an effective way to control another individual."[85]

Despite the fact that many abused children become adults who retaliate against their elderly parents, some retaliate at a much younger age. In "Why Kids Kill Parents," Kathleen M. Heide states that in the United States, incidents in which parents are murdered by their children occur nearly every day.[86] Contrary to popular belief, "in the great majority of cases, the child who killed was a white male," and most of the kids who murdered their parents "are neglected and abused children whose options are limited—children who honestly think they have no other way out."[87] When they become teenagers, they are more likely to kill because normal teen problems plus being abused push some over the edge. In another study she conducted, Heide learned that half of the female sexual abuse victims said that before age 18 they had considered murdering the abusive parent, and some had done more than just think about it; they had actually made plans to murder the parent. The solution to this problem is simple, Heide said, and it's the same message that I've been attempting to convey throughout this chapter: better parenting practices.[88]

A Brighter Day:
How Parents Can Help African American Youth

A Final Word

As I was writing this book, I celebrated a milestone birthday. Each year when my birthday arrives I'm reminded of the fact that my life is more than halfway over. Of course, as I grow older, I want my life to get better. I want to be able to enjoy myself. This includes enjoying the company and accomplishments of my children. As I get older, I will hopefully become wiser. But no matter how much wiser I become, I can't deny the fact that eventually, my body will become weaker. Therefore, as I grow older, I don't want to have to look over my shoulder when my adult children are around, fearing that they may one day retaliate for wrongs I committed or an abusive cycle that I perpetuated. I want my adult children to be able to look at me and say, "Mom wasn't a perfect mom, but she was a good one. Yes, she made mistakes along the way, but we always knew that she had *our* best interests and *our* needs in mind when she disciplined us." I also want to know that my children will one day rear my future grandchildren in loving, supportive, uplifting, healthy homes. Parents shouldn't have to live in fear during old age, wondering if the child that they brought into the world might take them out one day with a bullet, knife, or blow to the head. So, I conclude this chapter with a quote from the American Psychological Association that I believe all parents need to keep in mind as we are rearing our children: "Every person—no matter how young or how old—deserves to be safe from harm by those who live with them, care for them, or come in day-to-day contact with them."[89]

Chapter 2

Nothing from Nothing Leaves Nothing: Why We Need Healthy Self-Esteem and Self-Respect

As I was thinking of all of the stories I wanted to include in this chapter, I remembered one that I heard more than 20 years ago when I was a young junior high school teacher. A middle-aged African American woman who was very religious, very strict, and very solemn shared it with me. Because she rarely smiled, some people assumed she was mean. Others thought that she was too religious, for whenever anyone greeted her she always replied, "Praise the Lord!" But on the day that she shared the following story with me, I learned that underneath that hard exterior lay a wounded soul, a mother who was tormented by several bad choices she'd made during her younger years. Most of these choices were rooted in two factors: She had grown up believing that she was ugly, and feeling ugly had caused her to have low-self esteem and little, if any, self-respect.

According to this woman, "I always knew that I was ugly, so when I grew up, I decided that I needed to have a pretty man on my arm!" In other words, she believed that dating or marrying a handsome man would make her feel better about herself. Long after she made this decision, she did indeed end up with a "pretty man." His skin was much lighter than her leather-colored skin, and unlike her coarse hair, his was naturally wavy. By the time that she snagged this handsome man, the woman already had two young children—a son and

A Brighter Day:
How Parents Can Help African American Youth

a daughter. But she married her pretty man anyway, moved him into her house, and eventually had a child by him.

One day she experienced a mother's worst nightmare; she learned that her pretty man had raped her seven-year-old daughter. Of course, she was outraged. She wanted him to pay for his evil deed. She wanted him to suffer, and she wanted him in jail. So, she went through the long, painful legal ordeal—almost to the very end. But at the last moment, she changed her mind. "I found out that they were going to give him a much longer sentence than White men who'd done worst things," she told me. Therefore, not only did she request that the charges against her pretty man be dropped, but she soon accepted his apology, convinced herself that he had changed, and allowed him to move back into her home.

For many years, it appeared that her pretty man had changed indeed. But the woman eventually learned that he hadn't changed at all. One day, when her daughter was a teenager, the girl tried to kill herself. Later, she confided to her older brother that on the day that she attempted suicide, if he'd come home just a few minutes earlier he would have caught their naked stepfather running out of her bedroom. The man had tried to rape her again, but the brother's unexpected arrival home had interrupted his plans. Instead of having to live with the constant threat of being raped again in her own home, the girl decided that death was a better option. So, she tried to kill herself.

When the mother concluded this story, she told me that since that time, several things had happened. The pretty husband had died. "Boy did he look bad when he died!" she declared. Her son was currently in prison and had become so "institutionalized" that he seemed happier in prison than out on the street. Her daughter, who had been raped at age seven

Chapter 2: Nothing from Nothing Leaves Nothing: Why We Need Healthy Self-Esteem and Self-Respect

and nearly raped again years later, had suffered from ongoing mental problems. She also hated her mother and refused to have any contact with her.

As I've thought of this story throughout the years I've often wondered how different things might have been if the woman had grown up having healthy self-esteem and self-respect. If she had grown up knowing her worth, accepting herself, and finding beauty within herself would she have deliberately sought out men who were outwardly handsome but possibly rotten inside? Of course, I'll never know the answer to this question, but this story taught me a lesson that pertains to the main message I want to emphasize in this chapter: Healthy self-esteem and self-respect have a lot to do with the choices we make. A child who grows up feeling worthless is unlikely to find any good within himself or herself and will probably act accordingly. A parent who grew up feeling unlovable won't be able to love a child who looks like her. She won't be able to teach that child to love and accept herself. In other words, as Billy Preston sang, "Nothing from nothing leaves nothing." A parent can't help her child grow up to become an emotionally and psychologically healthy individual if the parent is full of self-hatred, low self-esteem, and no self-respect.

In this chapter, I will share stories and strategies that emphasize this message, but before I do that, I want to define self-esteem and describe some of the causes and consequences of poor self-esteem, particularly for us as African Americans.

What is Self-Esteem?
There seems to be a lot of confusion about how to accurately define self-esteem. The experts agree that it entails more than just feeling good about ourselves. It's a lot more

A Brighter Day:
How Parents Can Help African American Youth

complicated than that. How we feel about ourselves should be positive, but it should also be based on reality and a number of other factors. Bell Hooks, the celebrated author of many books about African Americans, devoted an entire book to the topic of self-esteem among Black people. In *Rock My Soul: Black People and Self-Esteem*, she uses terms such as "self-acceptance," "self-respect," "emotional well-being," and a refusal to "self-sabotage" as definitions of self-esteem.[1] According to Nathaniel Branden, an expert on self-esteem, among other things, self-esteem includes being self-accepting and believing that ". . . success, achievement, fulfillment— happiness—are right and natural for us."[2]

There are several main differences between people with low self-esteem and those who have healthy self-esteem. "Individuals with low self-esteem typically focus on trying to prove themselves or impress others. They tend to use others for their own gain."[3] Some of the characteristics of people with low self-esteem are arrogance, a lack of confidence, self-doubt, fear of risk taking, refusal to take responsibility for one's actions, and contempt for others.[4]

Causes of Low-Self Esteem Among African Americans

Hooks makes it clear that from the time the first Africans arrived in the United States, Black people have struggled to develop healthy self-esteem. From slavery until the present time, many forces have made this an uphill battle. She identified eight factors that have made developing healthy self-esteem difficult for Black people: religion, racism, white supremacy, the media, the color caste system among Blacks, the devaluation of Black females, stereotypes about Black males, and dysfunctional family practices, especially shaming and the abandonment of Black children by their fathers.[5]

Chapter 2: Nothing from Nothing Leaves Nothing: Why We Need Healthy Self-Esteem and Self-Respect

Some Consequences of Low Self-Esteem

Obviously having healthy self-esteem is very important. Parents need to have it, and we need to help our children develop it. Research has shown that low self-esteem is linked to many problems, including "violence, alcoholism, drug abuse, eating disorders, dropping out of school, teenage pregnancy, suicide, and low academic achievement."[6]

Looking for Love in All the Wrong Places: Sexual Promiscuity, One Consequence of Low-Self-Esteem

As I was writing this chapter, I was reminded of one of my favorite former high school students whom I saw in a shopping mall one day. To protect her identity, I will refer to her as "Princess." For many years after I left the K–12 public school system, I had thought about Princess, prayed for her, and wondered how she was doing. So, that day in the mall, when she tapped me on the shoulder as I was leaving a toy store, I was thrilled to see her again and to meet her two adorable children. To the average passerby, she probably appeared to be an attractive, young Black mother with a baby in a stroller and an active toddler who was eager to explore the toy store. But I knew her beauty and calm demeanor hid a tragic past.

At the high school where I taught for 11 years, Princess had earned a bad reputation among her peers. The main reason was that she had repeatedly allowed herself to be disrespected by male students. A student once told me that she and her classmates had watched Princess and a male student having sexual intercourse in broad daylight near one of the school's portable classrooms. On another occasion I learned that Princess had allowed her new boyfriend to burn her genitals with a cigarette lighter. Although many of her peers ridiculed her and looked down on her, I understood the main reason for her lack of self-respect and tolerance of abuse by others: When she was six months old, her teenaged mother had tried to drown her. After that, Princess was forced to live with a grandmother who was too tired and worn out by life's ups and downs to be saddled with another child. She often reacted with anger and violence towards Princess. Consequently, Princess had been conditioned to believe that she was unlovable and unworthy of kindness.

That day in the mall, when I saw her for the first time in seven years, I admired Princess's handsome sons. I asked how she was doing and whether or not she had kept in touch with any of her former high school classmates. I learned that her grandmother had died, that she had limited contact with her mother, and her former best friend from high school was doing well. Princess said that she didn't plan to have any more children. She never mentioned the children's father or her marital status, and I didn't ask her. But I noticed an older man, possibly Latino, hovering nearby as if he were waiting for her. Before we parted I gave her my business card and asked her to keep in touch. Afterwards I wondered if she would be able to break the cycle that her grandmother and mother had passed on to her by not only loving her sons but teaching them to love themselves.

Abusive Cycles: Another Consequence of Low Self-Esteem

Another related consequence of low self-esteem, especially for females, is that they may become so desperate for love and approval that they may make very bad choices that harm themselves and any children they may eventually have. Like the woman I described at the beginning of this chapter and Princess, these women may gravitate towards abusive men. One of my former neighbors is a good example of this.

What I remember most about this young African American mother was that both she and her daughter were very beautiful, but I cannot recall seeing the woman smile or ever look happy. She usually looked depressed and spoke in a flat tone. Sometimes, she talked about her childhood and teenage years when she was growing up in the Midwest. From all of the stories that she told me, I can only remember one. It's a story about her mother's boyfriend, a man who lived with my neighbor's family while she was growing up.

During my neighbor's childhood, her mother would allow this man to "discipline" her, even though she wasn't his biological child. The discipline often involved brutal beatings. When she became a teenager, the mother's boyfriend found a new way to humiliate her. Before each beating, he would force her to take off all her clothes. Then he would tie her to a chair and beat her with an extension cord. As I visualized how painful and degrading this must have been for her, I couldn't help but ask, "What did your mother do when he beat you?" "She let him," the woman replied calmly. Unfortunately, her story isn't unusual. Like many women, her mother's own low self-esteem contributed to her decision to allow a man to abuse her daughter, and unfortunately, the daughter might even end up passing on this pattern to her own child.

The Daddy Dilemma: Another Consequence of Low Self-Esteem

As Princess's story illustrates, low self-esteem can also lead to promiscuity and the mistaken belief that sex and love are the same thing. One of the consequences of so many Black

A Brighter Day:
How Parents Can Help African American Youth

teenagers and women becoming pregnant in their search for love is that way too many African American children grow up without having a father at home, and this can become a generational cycle. Boys who grow up without a dad in the home may grow up believing that it's normal for males to create babies and walk away from them. Many of the problems Black males and females face in the United States stem from this one problem.

In 2005, the article "Why Our Black Families are Failing" appeared in the *Washington Post* and was emailed to me by a friend. The article, written by William Raspberry, reported that Pentecostal ministers and members of the Seymour Institute for Advanced Christian Studies had recently met and concluded that the main cause of Black family failure is the absence of fathers in the home, and declining marriage rates. According to Raspberry, "Father absence is the bane of the black community, predisposing its children (boys especially, but increasingly girls as well) to school failure, criminal behavior, and economic hardship, and to an intergenerational repetition of the grim cycle."[7]

Misogynistic Men/Women Haters: Another Consequence of Low Self-Esteem

An acquaintance of mine, a middle-aged African American woman, shared a troubling story with me about her teenage years. To protect her identity, I'll refer to her as "Portia." She had grown up in a family that consisted mostly of boys, so Portia had several older brothers. For some reason, two of them were very cruel to women. In spite of this, they were also very charming and quite popular with women. One of these brothers captivated women from all walks of life. When Portia was a teenager, her brother started dating "a beautiful

Chapter 2: Nothing from Nothing Leaves Nothing: Why We Need Healthy Self-Esteem and Self-Respect

school teacher." I have no idea what "magic" spell Portia's brother cast on this educated and attractive woman, but according to Portia, neither the woman's beauty nor her education could change his personality.

After dating the woman for awhile, before long, his charm turned to venom. First, he became controlling and then verbally disrespectful. Next, the violence began. On one occasion, Portia witnessed a brutal beating. Her brother assaulted the teacher and ripped open her blouse. But this wasn't enough to satisfy his rage and sadism: After ripping open her blouse, he made her leave the house and stand on a corner, as if she were a prostitute. "And you better not move until I tell you to!" he ordered. Like a puppy who had been whipped into submission, this beautiful and highly educated woman stood on the corner as passersby stared at her ripped blouse, bruises, and tear-streaked cheeks. After the ordeal had ended and her boyfriend gave her permission to come inside, the humiliation and pain weren't enough to make her leave him—yet. It would take more pain and more abuse before she finally mustered up the courage to do so.

After Portia told me this story, it bothered me for quite some time. I was reminded of a college classmate who said that during childhood she had once seen a naked Black woman hiding in the snow. The woman's husband had thrown her out of the house without any clothes on during winter. When my classmate and her young siblings passed by, the woman apologized to them for being naked. "Sorry, kids," she said sadly as she tried to cover her breasts and genitals with her hands. Unfortunately, similar cases occur often because a lot of boys who have low self-esteem grow up to hate and abuse women, and a lot of women with low self-esteem tolerate this abuse.

A Brighter Day:
How Parents Can Help African American Youth

The Journey to Healthy Self-Esteem and Self-Acceptance

The stories that I have presented in this chapter, clearly show that self-esteem is an important topic for African Americans to explore. As parents, we need to have healthy self-esteem so that we won't pass our baggage on to our children. Parents and other individuals who work with Black children need to help youth develop healthy self-esteem. Because of the many factors I've already mentioned, helping Black children develop healthy self-esteem is a difficult, though not impossible, job. The following recommendations can help us help our youth.

Starting at the Beginning: Teaching Children Not to Be Ashamed of Our Roots, Africa

Shortly before I left the United States for Africa in 1981 to become a Peace Corps Volunteer, the *Los Angeles Times* published an article about Africa. Although I've forgotten the main purpose of the article, I do remember a quote from it. Today, this statement stands out as clearly in my mind as it did when I first read it.

When asked what he thought about Africa, an elderly African American man was quoted as saying, "I'm glad my great granddaddy jumped on that slave ship long ago!" In other words, the horrors and degradation that the man's enslaved ancestors suffered were well worth the trauma they endured during slavery. When I first read the quote, I was disgusted and ashamed of his ignorance. Now, I have more compassion for him, and I'm less judgmental. After all, like most Americans, he was probably just as much a victim from constantly hearing negative things about Africa as the rest of us.

Chapter 2: Nothing from Nothing Leaves Nothing: Why We Need Healthy Self-Esteem and Self-Respect

Most Americans hear negativity about Africa and Black people from the media, and at school, students rarely hear any positive information about Africa. They are taught that AIDS came from Africa. They hear that there are cannibals, widespread poverty, drought, famine, and "tribal" warfare in Africa. They are presented with images of half-naked African "savages." They never hear about the great ancient civilizations of Africa or about the wealth and riches of Africa that compelled greedy Europeans to voyage thousands of miles to the "dark continent" in order to profit from its diamonds, gold, and many other resources. Therefore, it is little wonder that, like the elderly man who was grateful that his great granddaddy jumped on that slave ship, many African American youth and adults are ashamed of Africa. The media and our social studies and history classes have brainwashed us about Africa. Unlike Mexican Americans, who rarely see themselves reflected in school curricula at all but who can easily travel to Mexico—their parents' ancestral homeland—to see reality for themselves, most African Americans will never have the opportunity to visit their ancestors' homeland.

More than 20 years ago, I had the great opportunity to visit Africa, and I was often amazed by what I saw. Before I left the United States for Africa, several African Americans tried to talk me out of going. One woman warned me that I would get an incurable disease. A man told me I would be appalled by the sanitary conditions in Africa. On top of that, he said that I was too outspoken and that in Africa, an outspoken female could get into trouble. The funniest comment of all came from my great grandmother. As she stood on her porch in east Texas, Mama Putt asked me, "Girl, why you wanna go to Africa? I saw some Africans on TV one time, and they all had bad hair!"

A Brighter Day:
How Parents Can Help African American Youth

In spite of these warnings, my trip to Africa turned out to be one of the most educational and enlightening experiences of my life. I saw many problems in Africa. I saw poverty. I witnessed the effects of drought and government corruption. I even saw examples of modern-day slavery with my own eyes. But, from the moment our airplane landed at the airport in Bujumbura, Burundi, I also saw much beauty in Africa—from the physical beauty to the many lovely cultural and family traditions. During my nearly two years in Africa, which were mostly spent in Cameroon, I saw great pride in family life, respect for elders, a strong value placed on education, and I experienced hospitality from many people.

When I returned to the U.S. and eventually began teaching junior high and later high school, I shared stories and photos from Africa with my students. In nearly every single case, the students—African Americans and non-Blacks—were astounded. They had been brainwashed and filled with so many negative stereotypes about Africa that they had difficulty believing the new information. This didn't surprise me. Most adults are just as ignorant about Africa as my K–12 students were. And this includes Black folks!

Regardless of how widespread this ignorance continues to be, the fact remains that Africa is the ancestral homeland of African Americans. In order to develop healthy self-esteem, self-love, and self-acceptance, we must address our stereotypes, ignorance, and shame about Africa. One of the first lies that we must face comes from the myth that has been passed down through history: that Black people are cursed because we are descendants of Ham, one of Noah's sons. According to the King James Version of the Bible, Noah had three sons, Shem, Ham, and Japheth. Many people believe that Ham, who had four sons, was the father of the Black "race." The incident that has caused so much controversy and is the source of the myth that Black people were cursed by God occurred after the Great Flood when Noah cursed his grandson Canaan.[8]

The scriptures make it clear that Ham wasn't the one who was cursed. The late J. Vernon McGee, a White minister who authored many books about the Bible and hosted the *Thru the Bible* radio show, said that it's "absolutely absurd" to think that the "dark races" are cursed. "The Scripture does not teach it."[9] McGee said the Phoenicians, Hittites, Jebusites, Amorites, Girgashites, and Hivites were descendants of Ham's son Canaan. But the "Africans—the Ethiopians, the Egyptians, the Libyans, etc."—descended from Ham's son Cush, one of the three sons who weren't cursed.[10] So for centuries, Black people have been led to believe a lie. This lie, that we were cursed by God, was created and spread by people who wanted us to feel ashamed and unworthy and who wanted us to believe that they were superior to us and that we deserved to be their slaves and at the bottom of society.

It's time that we stopped believing this lie and other related ones, and begin to teach our children the truth. We are not cursed. We shouldn't be ashamed of Africa. If Africa was such a horrible and "savage" continent, why did the "superpowers" encourage so many of their White citizens to travel there? The answer, of course, is that Africa had a lot of resources that they wanted—including the hearty and resilient Africans who would eventually be enslaved and become our ancestors.

Furthermore, in order to develop healthy self-esteem in ourselves and our children, we must treat Africans better by being more respectful and making an effort to learn as much as we can about their culture, native countries, language, etc. We must stop repeating stereotypical comments about

A Brighter Day:
How Parents Can Help African American Youth

Africans, and we must stop thinking that we are better than they are. Thousands of first-generation African immigrants now live in the United States. They can become a great resource to African Americans. We can also read books about African history, the great civilizations of Africa, and the role the "superpowers" have played in destroying the African economy, which has resulted in widespread poverty, disease, violence, corruption, and other problems that the media are so quick to focus on. We can trace our African roots so that we and our children can learn more about our ancestors and history. As we learn, we will hopefully, stop believing all the negative media reports about Africa, and we will teach our children not to be ashamed of Africa. Instead, we will teach them about the beauty and resilience that we've inherited from our African ancestors.

Facing Our Own Baggage: Being a Work in Progress

Before we can help our children develop healthy self-esteem, we must face our own baggage about ourselves. We must deal with all of the issues and effects of self-hatred, and self-rejection that so many of us have carried since childhood.

Earlier, I said that parents who hate themselves will have a hard time loving children who look like them and who remind them of what they hate about themselves. Like so many African Americans, I grew up with a warped image of myself. In fact, I grew up believing that most people were better, smarter, and more attractive than me. Because of this, I often allowed myself to be victimized and used by people who took advantage of my ignorance and vulnerability. If I tried to describe all the folks who pretended to be my friend or who pretended to care about me but turned out to merely be users, haters, and opportunists, I'd have to write another book! But these people could only do what I allowed them to do. They took advantage of me because *I* made it clear that *I* felt that *I* was inferior to them. So, why shouldn't they agree and take advantage of the situation?

Today, I thank God that those days are over! My own journey from being an emotionally damaged and physically abused child to a college undergraduate who believed that Black women were cursed to the person that I am today, has taught me several lessons that can be helpful to other parents:

1. We need to face our own baggage.
2. We need to learn how to love and accept ourselves.
3. We need to find strategies to help our children.

The main lesson that I've learned throughout the years is this: "Since I have to live with Gail 24 hours a day, seven days a week, I might as well learn to love, accept, and nurture the person that I spend more time with than any other person on the face of this earth." The result of this long process has truly helped me to become my own best friend and to realize that I am not the horrible person that so many people said I was. I am a child of God. I am a good wife. I am a good mother. I am a good great aunt and was a good foster parent to my great niece who was living with me when I started writing this book. I am a good teacher. I am a good role model. In my heart I am determined to use the gifts, talents, and opportunities that God has given me to try to make this world a better place. And when life and toxic and jealous people try to convince me that I am ugly, worthless, too Black, too fat or too skinny, not smart enough, not good enough, and inferior, I can counter all of those negative attacks with the truth, and the truth always sets me free!

A Brighter Day:
How Parents Can Help African American Youth

Based on my own personal journey, I recommend the following strategies to parents and other individuals who work with African American youth:

- Develop a strong spiritual life.
- Know that you were created for a reason, that God doesn't make junk, and He doesn't have any step-children.
- Use positive self-talk on an ongoing basis to constantly remind yourself of who you really are.
- Make a list of affirmations from scriptures, self-help books, famous positive quotes, etc., and read them daily.
- Read self-help and self-improvement books on a regular basis.
- Make wise choices about who to date, marry, and expose your children and yourself to.
- Eliminate toxic people from your life (I'll say more about this later).
- Don't strive to be perfect, but strive to do your very best.
- Remember that forgiving yourself at the end of each day is extremely necessary.

As children grow, parents and others can also share these strategies with them.

We Must Deal with the Skin Issue

The color caste system among Blacks has historically helped to destroy the self-esteem of many of our people. It's obvious that in order to have healthy self-esteem as adults and in order to help our children develop healthy self-esteem, as African Americans, we must deal with the "skin thing." Some of us have very dark skin; some have skin that is brown, caramel colored, or some other variation between dark and light; others have very light skin, and some even have nearly white skin. Complicating matters even further, is the fact that

Chapter 2: Nothing from Nothing Leaves Nothing: Why We Need Healthy Self-Esteem and Self-Respect

skin tones within our families can vary among the various members. Regardless, we must learn to accept our color variations or we'll continue to have low self-esteem, prevent our children from developing healthy self-esteem, and pass on a negative generational cycle. Ideally, this acceptance should start at birth. If we wait until our children have already been ridiculed and verbally attacked about their skin tone, the job is going to be a lot harder. A former colleague told me the following story that emphasizes why we should help Black children accept their skin tone as early as possible.

This African American woman and I used to teach at the same high school. One day she brought her daughter to work with her. When I first saw her daughter, I was a bit surprised because she looked very different from her mother. The mother had caramel-colored skin and the daughter was ebony toned. After observing the daughter's behavior and having opportunities to chat with her throughout the day, I couldn't help but admire her. In fact, I wished that I had been as self-confident, articulate, and comfortable in my own skin during my youth as she appeared to be.

The next day, when I had a chance to speak with her mother, I said, "I was so impressed with your daughter. She walks around with a lot of dignity and self-confidence." Her mother didn't seem surprised at all. Evidently she was used to hearing compliments about her daughter. She smiled at me and replied, "That's because of what I started doing as soon as she was born. When I saw that my baby was dark skinned, I nicknamed her 'my black pearl.' All of her life, I've been telling her that she is beautiful and that she's my black pearl. Now it's gone to her head, and no one can convince her that she isn't one of the most beautiful women in the world." Then the mother laughed, clearly pleased that her strategy had paid off.

A Brighter Day:
How Parents Can Help African American Youth

Throughout the years, I've often thought about that attractive, self-confident, dark-skinned teenager and the strategy her mother used. From the moment of her birth, her mother began to wage an *intensive* and *strategic* battle to build this child up in a world that would try to destroy her. So, when the negative comments eventually came from the child's peers and others who couldn't see any beauty in blackness, the attackers failed to accomplish their goal. The child's mother had literally "brainwashed" her into believing the truth: She was fine the way she was, she was not inferior to anyone, and her black skin was indeed beautiful.

Here are some simple strategies that we can use to empower our youth:

- As parents, we must accept our own skin tone as not being inferior or superior to anyone else's.
- We must accept our children's skin tone no matter how light, dark, or different it may look from our own.
- From the moment of a child's birth, we must begin to build that child up, instead of rejecting him or her because the child is "too dark" or "too light," etc.
- We should never show favoritism among our children, especially because of the children's skin tone.
- We should teach our children to select friends based on personality and common interests rather than physical appearance.
- We should teach our sons and daughters to select potential dating partners and spouses based on personality, values, common interests, etc. rather than solely on physical appearance.
- We should stop toxic and "color-struck" relatives from making negative comments about our children's physical appearance.

Chapter 2: Nothing from Nothing Leaves Nothing: Why We Need Healthy Self-Esteem and Self-Respect

We Must Deal with the Hair Issue

When she was four years old, my great niece Jayda, who was living with me at the time, often came home from preschool complaining about some of her classmates. "Robert said he didn't like my hair," she told me. On another day she said, "Isis said my hair is ugly." On still another day, she whined, "Why can't I wear my hair down?" Her complaints taught me two things: First, peer pressure starts as soon as kids begin to interact with other children their age. Jayda was only four, but her peers were already trying to influence her self-image. Second, she believed what they said was true. Although she has a wonderful head of thick black hair that I spent a lot of time parting, twisting, and decorating with colorful barrettes and bows every single day, her peers were able to convince her that her hair was ugly.

When Jayda first began to tell me about these insults, I was outraged. After all, they were criticizing the masterpieces that *I* had created on her head! I told Jayda not to listen to them. They didn't know what they were talking about, and they were just jealous. But one night, while I was blow drying her hair that I'd just washed, I thought of another approach: "Every time, Isis, Robert, or anyone else tells you that your hair is ugly, tell them, 'My hair is beautiful. God gave me beautiful hair.'"

The next morning, as I was combing her hair for church, I asked, "What are you supposed to say when someone says that your hair is ugly?" She shrugged her shoulders and replied, "I don't know. I forgot." So, I made her repeat after me, "My hair is beautiful. God gave me beautiful hair." I realized I would have to practice this message with her on a regular basis until she learned to believe it and until those words became a natural part of her thoughts and conversation.

A Brighter Day:
How Parents Can Help African American Youth

Like Jayda, most African American children learn at an early age that they have either "good" hair or "bad" hair. Many of us who were told that we had "bad" hair have suffered from having straightening combs and chemicals burn our scalps. During the 1960s, natural hairstyles became popular, and more and more Black people began to accept their hair as God gave it to them—long, short, jet black, light brown, sandy-colored, extremely curly, coarse, or straight. Unfortunately, low self-esteem still causes too many of us to pass along hair issues to our children. These issues can damage their self-esteem.

To help children learn self-acceptance, parents can use the same role-playing strategy that I used with Jayda. In addition, I recommend the following strategies:

- Read children's books that feature Black children and that contain good story lines to children.
- Surround children with lots of Black art that features all types of different hairstyles.
- Teach children how to respond if someone criticizes their hair.
- Compliment children as often as possible.

We Must Deal with the N Word Issue (and Other Forms of Verbal Abuse)

The average Black person is more likely to hear the N word roll off the lips of another Black person than a non-Black person. The N word has generated controversy for a long time, but the fact of the matter is that if Black people would stop using the word, it would lose its popularity. I believe that African Americans should stop using the N word, and teachers shouldn't allow students to use it. For me, the bottom line is that the N word is not a nice term, its use has damaged many African Americans, and Black people who use it tend to be hypocritical; they say it's okay for other Blacks to use the N word, but they become offended when non-Blacks, especially Whites, use it.

I've been called the N word by people who claimed to love me, but when they used this term I didn't feel loved. I have watched African American children react to being called the N word by a parent or so-called loved one, and I never saw any child appear to be happy at that moment. In fact, I believe that using it to refer to children is one of the main ways that parents can damage children's self-esteem. Because of my experiences, I promised myself that I would never refer to my children by this term, and I kept my word. After all, why would I want to call someone that I love a name that was created and widely used by people who hated Blacks? Therefore, I urge all African American parents to not only eliminate the N word from your vocabulary but to make a vow to never use it to refer to your children.

Here are some recommendations that I hope you will keep in mind the next time you are tempted to use the N word:

- If you were called the N word during childhood by family members, remember how you felt at the time.
- If you have ever been called the N word by non-Blacks, remember how you felt at the time.
- Keep in mind that the last thing that Black children need from their parents is to be verbally abused at home or anywhere else. Being called the N word and being cursed at are great ways to develop low self-esteem.

We Must Deal with the Sex Issue

It's a harsh but true fact that there are too many unwanted African American children in the United States. Some of the statistics I presented in the Introduction emphasize this point.

A Brighter Day:
How Parents Can Help African American Youth

One of the reasons why so many African Americans have low self-esteem is because many of us grew up feeling that we were unwanted and unloved by one or both parents, often a father. Some absent fathers were merely looking for sex from a girl or woman who was looking for love to improve her low self-esteem, but the end result was a baby, one the male never wanted, never expected, and may never claim or support.

The message that sex and love aren't the same thing is one that we African American parents need to remember and teach our children, starting at a very early age. Our youth are bombarded with messages promoting sex through TV, the Internet, music, and peer pressure. When children and parents believe that having sex will solve their problems, they may end up with sexually transmitted diseases, such as AIDS, or unplanned pregnancies.

The message that "Sex and love aren't the same thing," is one that every African American parent needs to remember and teach to their children, starting at a very early age. The second strategy that I recommend is for parents to be honest with their children. For example, I never hid the fact that I became an unwed single parent after I graduated from college. My daughter was three years old when I married my husband, who later adopted her. I always told her about the circumstances of her birth, answered any questions that she had, and when my other two children were older, I explained it to them. I also told my three children that I hoped that they would learn from the unwise choice I made and make better choices themselves. Even though I had a college degree when I became a single parent, I told them that my road had still been hard, and it had been difficult for me to raise a child alone for those three years before I got married. In fact, at one point things got so bad that I actually considered suicide.

Chapter 2: Nothing from Nothing Leaves Nothing: Why We Need Healthy Self-Esteem and Self-Respect

Being honest with our children and speaking candidly to them about the consequences of becoming sexually active are two strategies that I highly recommend. However, I also caution parents to refrain from using scare tactics. I was reminded of this point when I thought of a Pentecostal pastor whom I knew during childhood. When I was a teenager, he preached about sex during one of his sermons. He told the story of two individuals who were having illicit sex. Supposedly, they got stuck together and had to seek help to get unstuck. Their sin was exposed because they had to move around naked together in public before they could be separated. However, this scare tactic didn't work because at least two of the minister's daughters became teen parents.

Instead of using scare tactics, I recommend that parents consider using the following strategies:

- Be a positive role model. It's hypocritical to preach abstinence while exposing youth to inappropriate behaviors (e.g., letting "significant others" move into the home, making the kids call boyfriends "daddy," and exposing children to a parade of sexual partners in the home).
- Teach children that sex and love aren't the same thing.
- Teach children that some people will try anything and say anything in order to get them to have sex with them.
- Teach children why it is so important to treat their bodies respectfully (e.g., so that others will treat them respectfully, so that they will avoid sexually transmitted diseases, and so that they will avoid having unplanned pregnancies.
- Teach children that girls who become sexually active and get a reputation of being promiscuous will have a hard time earning respect.

- Teach girls that the same boy or man who might be whispering "I love you" in their ear today might be calling them "whores, sluts, hoochies," etc. on national TV tomorrow.

A Final Word

No matter what we do as parents and no matter how hard we try to shield our children from problems, it's inevitable that they will experience heartbreak at some time or another. At the extreme end of the heartbreak continuum are children who, through no fault of their own, are thrown to the wolves— evil, abusive, and disgusting adults who should never ever be given access to children. For children who experience multiple traumatic events, the road to developing healthy self-esteem will be much harder.

But even children who have an easier life will face heartbreak. Most will face some type of rejection or another. Most will have to deal with bullies at some point or another. Most will have to deal with racism, and many will be told that something is wrong with their physical appearance. When a child's self-image is assaulted, the last thing that he or she needs is for a parent to ignore the problem or add insult to injury by verbally abusing the child. Because the average African American child will face many storms throughout childhood, adolescence, and young adulthood, it is crucial for parents to start the self-esteem building work that I've discussed in this chapter as early as possible. As Ben Carson, one of the most famous African American neurosurgeons in the world, wrote, "parenting [is] life's most important responsibility."[11]

Chapter 3

To Hate or Not to Hate—
An Ongoing Dilemma for African Americans:
How We Can Help Youth Cope With Racism
and Fight Injustice

In early 2007 during a telephone conversation with my mother, I mentioned that I had been dealing with racism at work. Instead of being surprised, my 72-year-old mother replied, "You're going to have to deal with racism from now until the day you die. Elder Cooper just talked about that in church last Sunday." My mother and her pastor are right: In spite of America's recent historic presidential election, racism is alive in the United States, always has been, and it probably always will be. In *Black Families in Therapy: Understanding the African American Experience*, Nancy Boyd-Franklin, an African American therapist, says that racism is harmful, and it affects the lives of African Americans from birth until death.[1] In the previous chapter, I stated that racism is one of the main reasons why many African Americans develop low self-esteem. But racism can do a lot more than that. It can destroy one's health and even lead to death. Researchers have found that many African Americans, especially males, develop high blood pressure because of their ongoing exposure to racism. Others have found that racism can cause depression and mental illness.[2] In other words, as Dr. Alvin Poussaint said, "racism can destroy us as individuals."[3] Of course "us" includes our children—our legacy, our future.

Because knowing how to deal with racism effectively can become a life or death matter for our youth, every African

A Brighter Day:
How Parents Can Help African American Youth

American parent has a moral obligation to teach African American children how to identify racism, how to cope with it, and how to find the resources they will need to use when necessary. In this chapter, I describe several strategies that parents and other adults can use to teach children how to deal with racism.

Start As Early As Possible.

One of my African American graduate students said that during her childhood, her parents never taught her anything about racism. Her parents were born in California and just never bothered to teach her or her siblings what lay ahead of them. According to Boyd-Franklin, because of their belief that the civil rights movement would eliminate racism, many African American parents adopted a similar attitude. Sadly, as a therapist, Boyd-Franklin learned that when parents fail to teach their children how to deal with racism, often these children grow up to need therapy as adults.[4]

So it's not an option: We must teach our children about racism. But when is the best time to start? Of course, babies and toddlers are too young to understand anything about racism, but should preschoolers and kindergarteners be taught, or are they too young also? In my opinion, racism training should depend on the maturity and developmental level of the child. According to Drs. Comer and Poussaint, parents should discuss race with their children "in an easy and natural way."[5] For example, because her birthday arrives in late December, my great niece Jayda was still in preschool when she turned five. In January, to commemorate Dr. King's birthday, her preschool teacher taught the children about Dr. Martin Luther King Jr. and the civil rights struggle. Jayda would come home and tell me what she'd learned about Dr.

Chapter 3: To Hate or Not to Hate—An Ongoing Dilemma for African Americans: How We Can Help Youth Cope With Racism and Fight Injustice

King, and sometimes she asked me questions about White people. I chose to be as honest as possible with her. Because her maternal grandmother is White, I had to make it clear to her that *some*, not *all* White people, treated and continue to treat African Americans badly. I also read a book to her about Dr. King's childhood and his work, and answered her questions about the book.

Sometimes, parents are forced to talk to preschoolers about racism because their child has been rejected by his or her non-Black peers. Drs. Comer and Poussaint emphasize that parents should first make sure that the rejection is based on race, and then they should explain to their children that sometimes certain individuals won't want to play with them or associate with them. Parents can also talk to all of the children involved about how to play fairly and why it is important to let all children participate, etc.[6]

In two studies that I conducted with African American teenagers, the majority said they had experienced racism, particularly at school.[7] In another study that I conducted with African American college students, racism and discrimination were the most frequently cited obstacles the participants experienced during childhood or adolescence. The average student who experienced racism or discrimination during childhood said it occurred when the student was 13 years old. Children who were older at the time of their first racist experience were more likely than younger children to say that the incident(s) had a strong effect on them.[8] In another study that I conducted with African American parents, nearly 30 percent said their children had experienced racism at school, and "children were more likely to experience racism during elementary school as opposed to middle school or high school."[9]

A Brighter Day:
How Parents Can Help African American Youth

These studies suggest that parents really should begin to use some of the following strategies *before* children begin kindergarten. As parents, we should use caution and wisdom in determining which strategies are age appropriate, and you might need to modify some of the strategies in order to truly help your children deal with racism.

Teach Children How to Identify Racism.

It is important that we teach children *how to identify* racism. Just as many Whites are in denial about the existence of racism, many African Americans are often confused about what constitutes racism. This makes it easier for Whites to accuse us of "playing the race card." I hate this saying because it's an easy way for Whites to ignore legitimate claims about racism. One problem is that racism is so common in the United States that sometimes it's difficult for us to know when a bad experience that we've had or something that we've witnessed stems from racism or some other reason. The following story illustrates this point.

One afternoon, I was in a beauty supply store when I witnessed an interesting conversation. The elderly White woman who was at the front of the check-out line in which I stood kept questioning the cashier about her bill. She did this three times, but the cashier, a Latina who appeared to be in her mid-twenties, never raised her voice and never became defensive. Instead, she patiently explained how she had calculated the amount that was printed on the receipt.

While the cashier was patient, my own reaction was less positive. Because I was in a hurry, my impatience grew with each question the elderly woman asked. There was one cashier and one check-out line, and the elderly woman's repeated

Chapter 3: To Hate or Not to Hate—An Ongoing Dilemma for African Americans: How We Can Help Youth Cope With Racism and Fight Injustice

questioning kept me and the customers behind me from getting our own items rung up.

After what seemed liked eternity, but in reality was no more than five minutes, the elderly woman appeared to be satisfied that the cashier had charged her appropriately. Then, she thanked the cashier and issued an apology that troubled me for the rest of the day. "I'm sorry if I seem scatterbrained today," she said, "but my grandson's about to have brain surgery and it's hard for me to concentrate." Because I had been assuming that the White woman was nitpicking merely because the cashier was a Latina, after hearing her apology, guilt overwhelmed me.

Obviously we can't read people's minds, and there's no way of knowing if a person's bad behavior stems from racism or not. However, as parents we can prepare our children for the real world by teaching them the difference between racism and rudeness or disrespect. Some people just aren't nice people, or maybe they're having a bad day.

At the very least, we can help our children learn the differences between prejudice, racism, and discrimination. According to racism expert Dr. Derald Wing Sue, racial prejudice is a negative bias against an entire racial group that is based on stereotypes and generalizations. "Racial discrimination is any action that differentially treats individuals or groups. . .based on prejudice."[10] Racism is caused by policies, structures, and actions that keep racial groups at a lower level or status in society by people who are in positions of power.[11] Although anyone—including African Americans—can be guilty of prejudice, only Whites can be racist according to Wing Sue because in the United States, Whites are the only group who have the power to carry out discriminatory practices on a widespread level. At least Whites used to be the only group that could do this. Now that America has elected its first Black president, there is at least one Black individual in the U.S. who has the kind of power that Wing Sue associates with racism.

Teach Children the Importance of Paying Attention to Their Internal Radar System.

Parents must also teach youth that the racism of today is very different from the type of racism that was common before the civil rights movement. Back then, blatant forms of racism, such as George Wallace openly barring Black children from White schools, police spraying Black demonstrators with water hoses and siccing dogs on them, and widespread public use of the N word, were common. Although blatant acts of racism still occur, today the new and more common form of racism is the "color-blind" type. It's more covert and extremely subtle. In *Racism Without Racists*, researcher Eduardo Bonilla-Silva says that color-blind racism is a common ideology among Whites. This ideology consists of the ways in which Whites explain, justify, and make excuses for the privileges, advantages, and opportunities they are likely to receive merely because of their race.[12] Wing Sue said that color-blind racists usually aren't even aware that they're racist. Nevertheless, although the harm they cause may be unintentional, it can be even more damaging than blatant acts of racism.[13] One of the best ways to teach children how to detect color-blind racism is to teach them to listen to their "internal radar system."

In *The Gift of Fear*, Gavin De Becker simply refers to this internal radar system as "intuition," something everyone has. DeBecker is correct; every child is born with this internal radar system. Unfortunately, people, especially females, are conditioned to ignore their intuitive messages by being told

Chapter 3: To Hate or Not to Hate—An Ongoing Dilemma for African Americans: How We Can Help Youth Cope With Racism and Fight Injustice

that it's all in their heads, they imagined it, or they have no scientific proof to support their suspicions. DeBecker says our intuition sends us 11 signals, and we need to pay attention to them: fear, apprehension, suspicion, hesitation, doubt, gut feelings, hunches, curiosity, nagging feelings, persistent thoughts, and anxiety.[14]

Concerning racism, Wing Sue says that people of color should follow their instincts. Because we have had to study Whites in order to survive in the United States, most of us have learned some things about them that can help us deal with racism. Wing Sue refers to this as "the ability to see beyond the obvious..."[15] The following recommendations are based on Wing Sue's work:

- Pay attention to what your intuition (internal radar system) tells you about racism and the motives and behaviors of others.
- Don't let anyone convince you that you are imagining things or that your suspicions are wrong.
- Teach your children to trust their instincts.

Explain Why People Become Racists.

Another simple but important strategy is for parents to explain to children why people become racist in the first place. A White graduate student once asked me during a class break, "Isn't it true that people just want what's best for their own race?" I replied, "In my opinion, people with a superiority complex are just trying to hide the fact that deep down inside they feel inferior to other people." My answer angered him so much that he stormed out of class and never returned. However, Wing Sue's research shows that I was correct. According to this racism expert, people hold on to negative stereotypes about other groups because these stereotypes make them feel better about themselves and their own race. In other words, they need to feel superior to someone in order to feel good about themselves. Even when they are given information that shows that their stereotypes are wrong, some people will continue to hold on to them because their self-image is strongly linked to the need to look down on others.[16]

The student who walked out of class that day was also correct: One of the main reasons why many White people are racist is because they benefit from the institutional racism on which this country's socio-economic system is built. In fact, Wing Sue identified 20 privileges that Whites automatically have that people of color don't have. Even though most Whites will deny that they receive special treatment and opportunities from society simply because of their skin color and physical features, the truth is that they do have a "legitimate" reason for wanting the current racial hierarchy to remain as it is.[17] Therefore, it's much easier for many to become and to remain racist throughout their lives.

Another reason why many White people become racist is that they are socialized to view people of color, especially African Americans, as inferior to themselves. Children learn their first racist views from their parents. Even when White children want to interact with children from other racial backgrounds, their parents, grandparents, older siblings, and other relatives may prevent them from doing so. The church, media, school curricula, and peers also contribute to this racist socialization pattern. Psychiatrists agree that most racist behavior is "learned" behavior.[18] According to Carl Bell, an African American psychiatrist, "Probably 90 percent of racist behavior is learned."[19]

A third reason why a White person may become racist is because of a bad experience he or she had with a person of

Chapter 3: To Hate or Not to Hate—An Ongoing Dilemma for African Americans: How We Can Help Youth Cope With Racism and Fight Injustice

color. In "Finding the Reasons for Prejudices," a *Philadelphia Tribune* article published in 2006, Tom Martinez says that being harassed at the predominantly Black and Latino high school he attended turned him into a racist. "At one point, Martinez said, he was the only White kid at [his high school]... As a result, he was picked on often, and he developed hatred for African Americans because of his experiences. Martinez felt alone and vulnerable, and he fell into socializing with people in white supremacist organizations who made him feel important and strong."[20]

One of the most controversial theories about why people become racist is the theory that racists are mentally ill. Although most White psychiatrists have been reluctant to explore this possibility, several highly respected African American psychiatrists believe that this is a legitimate theory. For example, Dr. Alvin Poussaint said racism isn't always a sign of mental illness, but sometimes it can be. He said racists tend to display some symptoms that are associated with mental illness, such as "paranoia," "fixed beliefs," and "projection."[21] Dr. Carl Bell agrees that most racists may not suffer from mental illness, but it is "possible for racism to also be a symptom of a psychiatric disorder."[22] UCLA professor Edward Dunbar "has done research that indicates that there is a scientific basis to classify racism as a mental illness."[23] Tom Martinez, the former White supremacist, agreed that racism is a form of mental illness. According to Martinez, "It helped me tremendously to get counseling... People can change if you just give them a chance. Sometimes they need for others to open the door for them," he stated.[24] Today, in addition to giving talks throughout the nation about his experiences, Martinez also helps the FBI identify hate groups.

A Brighter Day:
How Parents Can Help African American Youth

Martinez's story is heartwarming and insightful because it's rare for African Americans to get a chance to hear blatant racists—who eventually changed their ways—talk about their experiences. Although my own experiences and research have convinced me that most racists will go to their graves unchanged, his story should provide a glimmer of hope to individuals who believe that people can change. In addition to explaining the theories about why people become racists, Martinez's story is one that parents may want to share with children.

Encourage Children to Choose Friends Based on What They Have in Common, but Also Teach Them to Be Wise and Discerning.

When my children were growing up, I never told them that they could only have African American friends. I wanted them to select friends based on what they had in common, such as a similar value system. Because they attended a predominantly White Christian elementary school, each of my three children ended up having friends from different racial backgrounds. For several years, my son's two best friends were an African American boy named Chatz and a White boy named Bo. As my children grew older, they continued to have friends from different backgrounds, but over time, pressure from their peers to only have African American friends increased. Their non-Black friends also experienced similar pressures from members of their own race.

My cousin used a similar approach with her children. When her daughters were growing up in South Carolina, she permitted them to select the friends that they wanted to have, regardless of race. As they got older, she told her girls that their White friends would eventually be pressured to stop being

their friends. This is exactly what happened. According to
my cousin, even though her daughters had close White friends
during elementary school, by high school, as a result of peer
pressure, some of their former White friends wouldn't even
speak to them.

I know of other African American parents who used a
different approach. Because of the prevalence of racism in
the United States, these parents believed that it was naïve for
them to teach their children that it was okay to have White
friends. One woman was so convinced that Whites were evil
and couldn't be trusted that she raised her son to have these
beliefs. Another woman said that a story her father shared
with her during childhood caused her to use a similar approach
with her firstborn child.

This woman's father had grown up in the South, and during
his childhood his best friend was a White boy. When the White
boy turned 13, he came to his African American friend and
said, "My father said that you have to call me 'Mister' now,
and I can't be your friend anymore!" The Black child was so
devastated by this betrayal that from that point on, he stopped
trusting Whites. Later, when he had children of his own, he
taught them not to waste their time thinking that they could
ever have true White friends. Consequently, when she had
children herself, his daughter did the same thing with her
firstborn child.

Because she valued education, she sent her son to an elite,
predominantly White private school. She told him he was
going there for "an education, and not to make friends." Since
she wouldn't permit him to have White friends, and most of
his classmates were White, the child was often lonely. Her
son's experiences eventually convinced her that perhaps this
wasn't the best approach to use with children. Therefore, when

A Brighter Day:
How Parents Can Help African American Youth

her other children were old enough to start school, she changed her approach, and allowed them to select friends of their choosing, regardless of race.

My own three children are adults now. Based on my own parenting experiences and what I've learned from other parents and research, I remain convinced that it is important for parents to allow children to choose friends based on similar interests and a similar value system—even if their friends are of a different race.

One of the advantages of allowing them to have friends from different racial backgrounds is that they will see that White people aren't superior to African Americans or any other group; they have their weaknesses, insecurities, and "baggage" like every other group. The danger of not permitting children to have friends from other racial backgrounds is that the off-limits group can become "forbidden fruit." The following story about one of my extended family members illustrates this point.

This particular relative of mine was reared by an African American mother who hated White people. She didn't believe they could be trusted, and she didn't believe they could ever be real friends with African Americans. Although her son grew up hearing his mother speak about "evil" White people, he ended up marrying a White woman. Despite the fact that he now has four children by three different women, the two children of whom he is proudest are the two that he fathered by the White woman.

This story should remind us that it is important to allow children to make friends across racial and ethnic lines. Teaching children that they can never be friends with non-Blacks can backfire. However, we parents should also inform our children that while it may be possible for them to become good friends with Whites and other non-Blacks, those individuals might still engage in cultural insensitivity by making offensive statements or asking offensive questions out of ignorance. They may also have relatives who are racist.

We should also inform our children that even though they may want to have friends from other racial backgrounds, many non-Blacks won't want to become their friends. This point is substantiated by research showing that most Whites don't want to live around African Americans, most Whites only have White friends, many Whites oppose interracial dating and marriage,[25] interracial marriages make up only a small percentage of the total marriages in the United States,[26] and many Whites continue to believe that the races should remain totally separated.[27] In spite of this, Drs. Comer and Poussaint agree that African American children should be allowed to have friends from all racial backgrounds. However, parents should become concerned if their children *only* want White friends, for this may be a sign of self-hatred and a lack of self-respect.[28]

Teach Them That Just Because a White Person Is Nice to Them, It Doesn't Mean that the Person Is Their Friend, and It Doesn't Mean that the Person Isn't Racist.

When it comes to dealing with White people, one of the most important lessons parents should teach children is that even though a White person smiles at them, is nice to them, and appears to like them, the person may still be a racist. This is a lesson that I've repeatedly learned from my experiences in the workforce.

A Brighter Day:
How Parents Can Help African American Youth

Teach Them How to Talk to White Folks in Positions of Power.

It's also important for parents to teach children how to talk to people who are in positions of authority. Since most of the positions of power in the United States are held by Whites, our children need to learn some important lessons about effective communication while they're young. In his book *Black and White Styles in Conflict*, Kochman said that one of the main reasons why misunderstandings often occur between African Americans and Whites is because Whites don't understand why many of us speak the way that we do. According to Kochman, most middle-class Whites learn to speak in a quiet, non-challenging, low-keyed, and non-emotional way, but many African Americans speak in an "animated" and "interpersonal" way that many Whites view as "confrontational." In other words, when we speak in a tone that is full of emotion because we feel strongly about what we're trying to say, a White person may assume that we are angry and attacking him or her. A White person may not understand that the emotion in our voice is there because we are trying to persuade the listener to agree with us. In fact, we may not intend to come across as oppositional, and we may not even be angry at all. In cases where a conversation stems from an initial disagreement, the White person may assume that the Black person doesn't really want to resolve the problem and that he or she is simply being argumentative. [29] Therefore, we must teach our children how to speak clearly and focus on the message that needs to be shared.

Another important point is that even though most Black people speak Ebonics or "Black English" when we are with other African Americans, most Whites equate the use of

Ebonics with ignorance and a lack of education. When dealing with adults at school, in public, and in the workplace, it's important for our children to understand that they should use standard English.

Our youth also need to know that most Whites expect us to be loud, demanding, and angry. Therefore, it can definitely be in our children's best interest to learn the following points:

- Be as polite as possible when speaking in public and with people in positions of authority.
- Use standard English when dealing with authority figures.
- Try to speak calmly and in a non-emotional manner in order to be taken seriously and so that White folks won't assume that you are being argumentative.
- When necessary, pray silently and take deep breaths to calm yourself down. Anger is a natural emotion, and sometimes it is the only response that makes sense. It's how it's handled that matters. Children need to know appropriate ways to handle their anger. Teaching them to count to ten, pray, walk away from a situation, or write out their feelings before they react can help them calm down and think of appropriate ways to handle their anger.

Teach Them Not to Waste Time Seeking White Folks' Approval.

It is extremely important that we parents teach our youth that it is self-destructive and a waste of time to seek White people's approval. After all, even though Whites control the power structure in the United States, they aren't God, they don't have a heaven or hell to put us in, and they aren't the

A Brighter Day:
How Parents Can Help African American Youth

ultimate masters of our fates. Too often, Black people forget this and we make trying to please and seek the approval of Whites our top priority. A story from my childhood illustrates this point.

When I was a little girl, I loved combing hair. I would practice on my dolls, and when I got older, I twisted and braided my own hair into elaborate creations. By second grade, I had gotten good enough to not only comb my own hair but my two younger sisters' hair as well. By the time I was in sixth grade, it was my responsibility to comb my hair and my two younger sisters' hair before we left for school. Over time I became resentful of having to comb my sister Tammie's hair since she was only 14 months younger than me and just as tall as I was. I felt that she should be combing her own hair. Sometimes, I would retaliate by deliberately parting her hair crookedly and making her braids look ugly, hoping this would motivate her to learn to comb her own hair. But in the case of my baby sister, Franchell, I always made sure that her hair looked beautiful.

Because I was so good at combing hair, I also combed my hair and my sisters' hair on weekends. One Saturday, our entire family got dressed up to visit an elderly couple who had taken our family under their wings. From the time that my parents had first moved to California from Texas, this African American couple, whom my mother met at church, had served as mentors and role models to my mother. They were hardworking, owned their own home, and lived in a nice neighborhood. Because they were one of the few middle-class Black couples that we knew, and were considered to be pillars of the church, my family had a lot of respect for them, and their opinion mattered to us.

Chapter 3: To Hate or Not to Hate—An Ongoing Dilemma for African Americans: How We Can Help Youth Cope With Racism and Fight Injustice

So, on that Saturday when we went to their home, I was a little nervous about visiting them. I wanted to look my very best and made sure that Franchell's hair looked good. Unfortunately, the visit didn't go well for me. When we arrived at their house, as usual the couple greeted each one of us and commented on our appearance. They probably mentioned how tall some of us had grown or how nice some of us looked. But I really don't know for certain what they said or how long the visit lasted because only one moment and one comment remain frozen in my memory.

When the elderly woman turned to Franchell and demanded, "Who put all that grease in that baby's hair?" I froze in fear. I was horrified. I wanted to disappear or run out of her house. While I stood there wallowing in fear and shame, my mother blurted out, "Gail did it. Gail did her hair!" The elderly woman turned to me with a disapproving look and asked, "Honey, don't you know that that's what the White folks say about us, that we use too much grease and have greasy heads?" Guilt, shame, and embarrassment overwhelmed me. I felt that everyone in the room was looking at me as if I'd committed a crime. I had brought shame on my family in front of this respected couple. We already felt inferior to them; now I had ruined the visit.

I have never forgotten that incident or the related lessons I learned. One of the biggest reasons why so many Black folks are dysfunctional and have a shame-based personality is because we have spent way too much time worrying about what White folks think about us and our children. Over the years, I've learned that it doesn't matter if I wear my hair in braids, an afro, or straightened. It doesn't matter if my skin is jet black, caramel colored, "high yellow," or some other variation that indicates my African ancestry. It doesn't matter if I have a Ph.D., which I have. It doesn't matter if I've published numerous books, which I have. It doesn't matter if I rear my children to be God-fearing, highly-educated, law-abiding citizens, which I have. No matter what I accomplish, where I live, or how I look, most White people will believe that they are superior to me and that I am deficient in one way or another. Therefore, it would be stupid for me to spend my life seeking their approval and admiration. I will never please a group of people who refuse to see me as I am—a beautiful, talented, kindhearted child of God. Consequently, what God thinks of me has become the standard that matters most to me.

In her excellent book, *The Disease to Please: Curing the People-Pleasing Syndrome*, Harriet Braiker writes that "people pleasing" (which she refers to as the "disease to please") is "a serious psychological problem."[30] Although Braiker, a White woman, wasn't writing specifically for or about Blacks, many of her strategies and insights about people pleasing can be helpful to those of us who need to deal with our own problem of seeking White folks' approval. Only then will we be psychologically healthy enough to prevent our children from developing this problem. In the chapter called "Talking Yourself Out of Approval Addiction," Braiker reminds readers to remember the following points:

- No matter how hard we try, some people will still dislike us.
- Our self-worth shouldn't be based on winning the approval of others.
- We shouldn't make other people's racist baggage our problem.
- Approving of and accepting ourselves should be more important to us than the opinions of others.[31]

Chapter 3: To Hate or Not to Hate—An Ongoing Dilemma for African Americans: How We Can Help Youth Cope With Racism and Fight Injustice

Teach Them That God Doesn't Have Any Stepchildren.

In my research and workshops, I often say that "God doesn't have any stepchildren, but America does." By that I mean that America has historically treated people of color and low-income people like stepchildren. This status continues to plague African Americans and Latinos. Most White Americans, educators, and policy makers continue to view us as less deserving than Whites, and the policies and practices that are common in the U.S. indicate this to be true. Even though America may continue to view us as stepchildren, as I stated previously, "We are not cursed," and we were created in God's image, just as much as any other group of people. As parents, we must keep reminding our children that they are not inferior, they don't deserve second-class citizenship, and they must not believe the lies and stereotypes that continue to be spread about African Americans.

The easiest way for us to instill this message in our children is to constantly remind them of this. Long before children ever have their first experience with racism and teasing from peers, parents should already be telling them that God didn't make a mistake when He created them. When African American children complain about their skin color or question why they can't be White, parents can tell them that most White folks may view themselves as being superior and more attractive than African Americans, but when the sun comes out, many of them will risk getting cancer in order to darken their skin! Teaching children about Black people who have accomplished great success in this country and about ancient African civilizations is also important. Some Black parents teach their children that Jesus was described as having skin like bronze and hair like lamb's wool. The main point that parents need to remember is that if we allow our children to grow up feeling inferior, then in the long run, the racists and

A Brighter Day:
How Parents Can Help African American Youth

White supremacists will win, for the self-hatred, self-rejection, and low self-esteem that our children develop will be passed on to future generations of African Americans.

Teach Children Why They Must Fight Injustice.

One day, as I was standing in line waiting to be served at my local bank, I witnessed an incident that upset me. A poorly dressed elderly Black woman was waiting at the front of the line. Her gray hair had been braided in plaits that went in several directions, she wore a skirt that barely reached her ankles, and her dark, wrinkled face looked like it had seen many hard times. Her appearance reminded me of old photos of Black sharecroppers. As she stood in line, I noticed that several bank tellers appeared to be joking as if they were on a coffee or lunch break. As the minutes ticked by, not one of them acknowledged the waiting customer.

After awhile, the old Black woman began to grumble about the rudeness of the employees. I totally agreed with her. Apparently, when they realized what was happening—that two Black women who happened to be the *only* customers in line that day, were getting upset over their unprofessional conduct—one of the young White tellers eventually beckoned to the elderly woman and said, "I can help you, Ma'am." Another teller quickly offered to assist me with my transaction as well.

After the elderly woman concluded her business and slowly shuffled out of the bank and I finished my own business, I returned to my car. But, the incident continued to nag me. I could be wrong, but I didn't believe the tellers would've been so blatantly rude to an elderly White woman. So, I picked up my cell phone and telephoned the bank's headquarters. When I reached the customer service department I said, "I just left [the bank's name and branch location], and

Chapter 3: To Hate or Not to Hate—An Ongoing Dilemma for African Americans: How We Can Help Youth Cope With Racism and Fight Injustice

I want to complain about an incident that occurred." I explained that I was a customer at the bank and had watched an elderly Black woman being ignored as if she were unimportant. I stated that the tellers had behaved in a rude and unprofessional manner, and I described the tellers who were available at the time. The customer service representative appeared to take my complaint seriously and assured me that the branch manager would be contacted immediately. I believe that she kept her word, for since then I've noticed that all of the tellers at the bank behave more professionally, and they quickly assist waiting customers—even Black ones.

Experience has taught me that most people wouldn't have gotten involved in someone else's business to the degree that I did that day. But as I stood there watching that old woman being ignored as if she weren't worthy of respect and as if her money wasn't good enough, two points came to mind: First, that elderly woman could've been my mother standing there, being mistreated, and second, years from now, that could be me. If it were my mama or me who had been wronged, I would definitely want someone to speak up on our behalf. The day might come when I'm too old and too frail to fight for myself or too uninformed about the options that are available to force people to treat me correctly. Therefore, while I'm still relatively young and knowledgeable about the ways in which injustice can be fought, I have a moral obligation to speak out—even if it doesn't necessarily affect me directly. This is the legacy that we inherited from our great leaders of the past, including Thurgood Marshall, Dr. Martin Luther King Jr., Rosa Parks, Medgar Evers, Dr. W.E. B. DuBois, James Weldon Johnson, Ida B. Wells, Dr. John Hope Franklin, and countless other Black men and women who never became famous but who risked their lives and careers so that we could have a better life. This is also an important lesson that all Black

A Brighter Day:
How Parents Can Help African American Youth

children need to learn. Racism and injustice must not be ignored, taken lightly, or make us cower in fear. Each one of us must fight it.

Of course, a lot of people, including some Black folks, would disagree with me. Some African Americans have adopted the attitude that as long as no one is bothering them, or even if they're being treated unjustly, the best response is no response at all. This attitude gives people permission to mistreat others. In fact, history is full of examples of countless situations in which evil was allowed to thrive because people were too cowardly or too unconcerned to fight it. The following strategies are simple ways that we can empower our youth:

- Encourage youth to take appropriate action (depending on the circumstances) when they believe they have been subjected to racism or other types of injustice.
- Tell youth to inform you when someone has treated them unfairly.
- Teach them how to write letters of complaint to the appropriate person in charge.
- Teach them how to start a "paper trail" in order to document names, dates, places, and details about specific events.
- Teach them how to use the legal system and even file a lawsuit if necessary.
- Keep reminding them to always insist that people treat them respectfully and remember to treat others respectfully.
- Use storytelling to teach children how you have handled racism.
- Use "what would you do" scenarios to help children develop options when they are faced with various types of racism, such as being followed in stores, being

Chapter 3: To Hate or Not to Hate—An Ongoing Dilemma for African Americans: How We Can Help Youth Cope With Racism and Fight Injustice

harassed by police, being called the N word by non-Blacks, being treated unfairly by educators, seeing another person being treated unfairly, etc.

A Final Word: We Must Teach Our Children About Racism Without Making Them Bitter or Hateful.

During the spring and summer of 2005, I constantly found myself praying, "God please help me not to hate White people." At the time, my family and I were going through several particularly challenging ordeals. To some degree or another, all of these involved White people. The main lesson that I learned is one of the most important for African American parents to teach our children: No matter how much racism we experience, we must not become bitter or hateful. This is easier said than done, as the following story from one of my local newspapers illustrates.

The article, which was published in 2004, focused on a 10-year-old girl who had attempted to hang herself on her school playground. This African American fifth grader in a predominantly White affluent school district had chosen suicide as a way of escape after repeatedly being the target of racial slurs by her classmates. When her mother sued the school district for failing to put an end to the harassment, a jury refused to believe that the mother had made sufficient attempts to bring the problem to the attention of school officials. In other words, the mother was blamed instead of the school culture and the students who had repeatedly hurled racial slurs at the child. When the little Black girl learned of the trial's outcome, she said sadly, "They didn't believe me." Then, she tried to kill herself.

This story is a powerful example of why it is so important for us to arm our children with the tools they will need to deal

A Brighter Day:
How Parents Can Help African American Youth

with the racism that is so common in America. The bottom line is that racism can surface at any time, and no African American—from the young child to the older, seemingly wiser, more educated adult—is immune. It continues to be an ugly stain on America's history and present that we can't ignore. When we do so, we fail to prepare our children for the realities that they will inevitably face at various points in their lives. But of course, we must prepare our children without making them hateful and vengeful.

An African American woman who used to babysit for one of my daughters told me that when Dr. Martin Luther King Jr. was killed, her husband came home in tears. "He grabbed his gun and wanted to go and kill some White people," she said. Of course, she talked him out of it. If he had gotten his wish, he would've killed some White folks who had nothing to do with Dr. King's death, thus ruining his family's life and his own, for he probably would've been executed. Although anger is a legitimate response to racism and other forms of injustice, we do our youth a great disservice by not teaching them appropriate ways to handle their outrage. "Two wrongs don't make a right," and anger that results in violence against innocent people is wrong.

I will say more about racism later, but for now it is important for African American parents to remember the following:
- It's unwise for us to be in denial about the prevalence of racism in the United States.
- It's unwise for us to be ignorant about what racism is.
- We must teach our children how to identify racism, why it occurs, and options that they can use when they experience racism.
- We must teach age-appropriate strategies to children.
- We must emphasize to youth that becoming bitter and hateful is counterproductive.

Chapter 4

Seven Life Lessons That Can Empower African American Youth

In previous chapters, I described strategies we can share with African American youth that will help them have the bright future they deserve and become healthy and successful adults. There are lots of other skills and information that our youth need as well. Therefore in this chapter, I explain seven additional important life lessons and share related stories and strategies that we can use to empower our youth. The seven lessons are:

1. Teach youth how to deal with toxic people.
2. Teach them the difference between forgiving and forgetting.
3. Teach them that rejection is an unavoidable aspect of life.
4. Teach them that creativity can be a powerful coping tool.
5. Teach them that success is the best revenge.
6. Teach them to tithe.
7. Teach them to focus on the Big Picture.

Teach children how to deal with toxic people.
There are many types of people in the world. Some of the people we have to deal with make us better, and others affect us negatively. Those who have a negative effect on us fit into the group I call "toxic people," a term other writers have used. My simple definition is, "Toxic people make you feel bad about yourself after you've come into contact with them." Cheryl Richardson, an author and lifestyle expert, identified five types of toxic people: the blamer, the drainer, the shamer, the discounter, and the gossip.

A Brighter Day:
How Parents Can Help African American Youth

The blamer blames his problems on others. The drainer is a needy person who monopolizes other people's time and attention and constantly seeks advice, help, "or whatever she needs to feel better in the moment."[1] The shamer, according to Richardson, "may cut you off, put you down, reprimand you, or make fun of you or your ideas in front of others."[2] The discounter is argumentative, wants to be right, and doesn't appear to respect other people's opinions. The gossip, of course, talks about people behind their backs.[3] Interestingly Richardson makes her strongest statement about the shamer. "This person," says Richardson, "can be hazardous to your health."[4] I agree with Richardson but would add that all types of toxic people can be hazardous to our health and that of our children. Therefore, teaching youth how to deal with toxic people is one of the best ways to arm them with the tools they'll need to become healthy adults.

Each of us will have to deal with toxic people at some point in our lives. We can encounter them as bullies on the school playground, a racist teacher or professor, a boss or co-worker in the workplace, or even a family member. Because we can't pick our family members, dealing with toxic relatives can be a lot harder than dealing with other toxic people. Sadly, as I indicated in chapters 1 and 2, many children have toxic parents—parents who are destructive in one way or another. When children are forced to live in homes with toxic parents, it is very difficult—but not impossible—for them to become mentally healthy.

Before we can teach our children how to deal with toxic people, we must first deal with ourselves. The following self-assessment will be most effective if you answer the questions honestly:

Chapter 4: Seven Life Lessons That Can Empower African American Youth

- Is my child's wellbeing one of my top priorities?
- Do I try to keep my child safe from harm?
- Do I keep toxic relatives, friends, and acquaintances away from my child as much as possible?
- Am I a good role model? Do I demonstrate good values and morals through my speech and actions?

Second, we must do our best to keep toxic people away from our children. This starts in the home with the individuals that we allow to visit and live with us. One African American woman learned this lesson the hard way. This woman wanted to help her brother get his life together after he was released from prison. So she allowed him to move into the apartment she shared with her teenage daughter. One day, the woman went to work, leaving her daughter home alone with her brother. The daughter was doing her homework when her uncle called her into a back bedroom, claiming there was a phone call for her. He then attacked her and tried to rape the child. She fought back but ended up with a broken nose. Later, her distraught mother insisted that she didn't know that her brother had served time for a sex crime. She had believed him when he said that he'd been arrested for a non-violent crime. Because of her naiveté, her daughter may suffer for a lifetime. She brought the devil into her home, and the devil did what devils do; he acted evil and tried to destroy an innocent child.

Anna Salter, an internationally known expert on sexual predators, said predators view single mothers and religious people as the two easiest targets.[5] Because single mothers are often lonely, many let down their guard when men appear to be interested in them. Lots of examples come to my mind about such women, but the following story involves a woman that I never even met.

A Brighter Day:
How Parents Can Help African American Youth

Several years ago, I learned about this woman one day when I was at a local park with my great niece Jayda. I was sitting next to Jayda on a swing when I heard a high-pitched voice behind me squeal, "Oooh! She's soooo cute!" A few seconds later, a Black man rushed over to us and continued to rave about Jayda's beauty. Because he talked nonstop, I quickly learned that he had brought a six-year-old boy to the park to play. He pointed at a little Black boy who was riding a pink bike that he'd borrowed from another child in the park. As the boy zoomed by us on the bike, the man continued to talk. He informed me that although I'd permitted Jayda to wear sandals to the park, he would've never allowed the little boy to wear sandals to the park. "It's too dangerous," he explained.

As he chattered on and on, a red flag soon went up in my mind. It was the same red flag that had popped up when I first heard the man's voice without seeing his face. "I came all the way from Los Angeles to play with him," the man told me, "and I try to come every weekend to spend time with him. The mother and I aren't dating or anything, but I just *looove* spending time with him."

For a long time after that conversation ended, I kept thinking about this incident, and two questions came to mind. First, was the little boy's mother so naïve, overworked, and overwhelmed that she would allow a grown man to drive nearly 60 miles each weekend to spend time with a child to whom he wasn't biologically related or related to by marriage, for the child wasn't even his son? Second, was the mother fooling herself into thinking that this man—who wasn't even remotely interested in dating her—was really interested in her instead of her son? Without even meeting her, I sensed she was either knowingly or subconsciously willing to allow her son to be a pawn, and possibly even molested, in order to

86

have this man in her life. Unfortunately, lots of desperate women do the same thing in order to have a man in their lives.

Salter also mentioned that predators view religious people as easy targets. Religious people are vulnerable because they've been taught to focus on the good in people. As an individual who grew up in church, I've seen my share of toxic people in churches. I saw my older sister being criticized, ridiculed, and humiliated in churches when she was a little girl and a teenager.

I've also seen the damage done to lots of other people, such as a fellow teenager in one of the churches I used to attend. This girl was constantly pinned to the floor by several adults as they attempted to cast "demons" out of her. Another childhood acquaintance was walking home from school one day when a local pastor, who often visited our church, offered to give her a ride home. Because we'd been taught that ministers were representatives of God, this girl didn't think twice before accepting his offer. Later, when she told her family and church officials that the man had raped her, she was warned that she shouldn't make accusations against "the anointed man of God." After this horrible incident happened, I finally understood why that pastor's stepdaughters—two extremely beautiful teenagers—never smiled when I saw them at church and why they always looked so sad.

Another place in which children can encounter toxic people is at school. Bullying is a big problem in schools, and each year, we hear about cases of school violence. We also hear stories about teachers who sexually abuse their students and inflict other forms of abuse on children.

Workplace violence has also generated lots of media attention. In numerous instances, the person who went on a

A Brighter Day:
How Parents Can Help African American Youth

shooting spree at work was an individual who believed that he was being treated unfairly, harassed, or subjected to abuse from a toxic boss or co-worker.

Because all youth will have to deal with toxic people at some time in their lives, and possibly many times, it's wise for us to start preparing them early. In addition to dealing with any toxic behaviors, attitudes, or beliefs that we ourselves have, and doing our best to limit our children's contact with toxic people, we can use the following strategies:

- Teach children the difference between toxic and non-toxic people.
- Teach children that it's important to "follow their gut instinct," listen to their intuition, and pay attention to red flags about people.
- Teach them that it's important to avoid toxic people as much as possible.
- Teach children to avoid becoming toxic themselves, by not bullying others, following the behaviors of troublemakers, or criticizing and undermining others because of jealousy and insecurity.
- Don't uphold your child when he or she is wrong. If the child is guilty, it is important to teach him or her the difference between right and wrong. Hold the child accountable for wrongdoings.

Teach them the difference between forgiving and forgetting.

Long ago when I was a college undergraduate, I was horrified while watching television news scenes of hundreds of people—mostly Black folks—who had killed themselves and their children by drinking cyanide at the urging of their "spiritual" leader, the Reverend Jim Jones. If I remember

Chapter 4: Seven Life Lessons That Can Empower African American Youth

correctly, the sign hanging over their headquarters at the People's Temple in Guyana said, "Those who forget the past are destined to repeat it." Since that time long ago, when the news media shocked the world with coverage of the manipulation and other tactics Jones used to convince his followers that he was a messenger from God, I've often thought about that quote. I believe it's one that we parents should pass on to our children. We should also teach them that while it's important to forgive the people who have wronged us, forgetting the lessons that we need to learn from painful experiences is unwise and even dangerous.

Psychologists have repeatedly talked about the importance of forgiveness. Many say that forgiveness is necessary in order for us to be mentally and even physically healthy. Holding on to anger and grudges can make us physically sick. For example, researchers say that "harboring feelings of betrayal may be linked to high blood pressure which can ultimately lead to stroke, kidney or heart failure, or even death."[6] On the other hand, forgiveness has several benefits, such as reducing stress, helping us develop stronger relationships with others, helping our hearts to stay healthy, and creating more happiness and less pain for us.[7]

Evangelist and author Joyce Meyer often talks about forgiveness. Because she was sexually abused by her father throughout much of her childhood, Meyer held onto a lot of anger that eventually began to affect her relationships. Fearing that other people would take advantage of her caused her to become extremely controlling. Over time, however, she realized that in order to heal emotionally, she needed to forgive her parents. Meyer not only forgave them, but she was eventually responsible for their welfare during their elderly years.

A Brighter Day:
How Parents Can Help African American Youth

Although Meyer stresses the importance of forgiving people who have wronged us, she also does something that many people who preach about forgiveness don't do: She doesn't tell victims that they should *forget* what was done to them. In fact, in her books and sermons, she often speaks about her father's crimes against her as a way to help other wounded people. Meyer's honesty and openness about her past are two of the reasons why her books have become bestsellers and her ministry is so popular.

Like Meyer, I strongly believe that forgiveness is necessary for good health, and I also believe that forgiveness and forgetting aren't the same thing. Forgetting wrongs that have been committed can cause a victim to become victimized by the same person or in the same way again. Therefore, parents should consider using the following strategies to teach children about the difference between forgiveness and forgetting:

- Tell children explicitly what forgiveness means.
- Tell them why it's important to forgive.
- Teach them that it's important to remember what they learned from painful experiences.
- Teach them that apologies may be sincere, but they can also be insincere.
- Teach them that it's important to remember what Maya Angelou said: "When people show you who they are, believe them." In other words, if someone's actions show you that he or she is a devil, protect yourself from this individual.
- Teach them to look at patterns of behavior. If someone has a history of treating other people badly, don't assume his or her behavior will be different towards you.

Chapter 4: Seven Life Lessons That Can Empower African American Youth

- Teach them that the old saying, "Actions speak louder than words," is true.

I conclude this section with a story that explains why we should forgive but never forget. Many years ago, my friend Malinda, told me a fable that I've often shared with my children, students, and others. Evidently, she'd heard this story during her childhood, and different versions of it have been passed around for decades. This is a wonderful story to tell children because it emphasizes the need to forgive while also teaching that apologies can be insincere.

"The Cold, Cold Snake": A Story About Forgetting and Forgiveness

There once was a man who lived in a small cottage in the woods. The man didn't have a wife, children, or family members, so he was very lonely. Each day he followed the same routine. After waking up, getting dressed, and eating a simple breakfast, he trudged to a job that he hated. At the end of the day, he trudged back to his little cottage, ate dinner alone, went to bed, and woke up the next morning, only to repeat the same ole boring routine.

On a snowy winter evening when the man returned to his home, he noticed an object on his doorstep. As he leaned over to inspect it, he quickly realized that it was a small snake that apparently had frozen to death. The man picked it up, and just as he was about to throw the snake away, he felt it move. When he saw that the snake was actually alive, he rushed

A Brighter Day:
How Parents Can Help African American Youth

into his cottage, lit a fire in the fireplace, and stroked the snake until it had warmed up enough to begin to slither around. Because of his loneliness and the fact that the poor, little weak snake looked so harmless and needy, the man decided to keep it. So, he fed it, named it, and built a cage for it.

Finding the snake changed the man's life. Now he had something to look forward to. Each morning before leaving for work, he fed, stroked, and talked to his new pet. In the evening, instead of trudging home slowly, he now hurried. His pet needed him. Because of all of the love and care that he lavished on his pet, over time, the snake grew fat and became very healthy. The man loved his snake, and since he'd saved its life and took care of all of its needs, he assumed that the snake loved him too. But he was wrong.

One evening, when the man reached into the cage to feed his pet, the snake bit him. "Ouch! That hurt!" the man screamed, as he slammed the door of the cage. Blood dripped from his hand, and tears filled his eyes. "After all I've done for you—saved your life, fed you, took care of you, and loved you as if you were my very own child—how could you do this to me?" The snake looked at him and calmly replied, "But you knew I was a snake."

I love this fable because it contains several important messages that we can teach children. The first message is that "snakes" can charm us into loving them. Of course, I'm talking about snakes that walk on two feet—human beings who act like snakes. I've never been bitten by the reptilian type of snake that slithers on its belly, but I've been bitten numerous times by snakes on two feet: people I trusted, forgave, and believed when they said they'd never hurt me again. However, as soon as my guard was down, I had to nurse another "snakebite" because I mistakenly assumed that in order to forgive these individuals, I also had to forget and start over with a clean slate. Like the man who thought he could tame a snake and treat it as if it were a harmless pet, I too was wrong about these individuals.

A second message contained in the fable is that a snake can only be what it is: a natural enemy to human beings, and enemies don't have our best interests at heart. Even when we treat them nicely, their true colors eventually come out. People can change and become better if they really want to, but at the same time, I believe that once an individual has exhibited snake-like, dangerous, or predatory characteristics, caution is required *at all times* when dealing with that person. I also want to add something that the late Thurgood Marshall, the first African American Supreme Court Justice, said shortly before his death: A black snake can be just as deadly as a white one. In other words, although many African Americans grow up believing that they can't trust most White people, often our biggest hurts will come from family members, friends, and acquaintances—other Black folks.

Regarding "The Cold, Cold Snake" fable, I don't know what happened after the snake replied to the man's question, but we parents can use this story as a teaching tool for our youth. For example, we can ask children the following questions:

A Brighter Day:
How Parents Can Help African American Youth

1. If you were the man who had just been bitten by the pet snake that you loved so much, what would you do?
2. What could happen if the man decided to keep the snake as a pet?
3. What might happen if the man just forgave the snake and forgot about being bitten?
4. How should we treat people who have hurt us?
5. What are the main lessons that we can learn from this story?

We must teach our children that rejection can't be avoided.

Another important life skill that we should teach our children is how to deal with rejection. Rejection is an unavoidable fact of life. It can come from family members, friends, teachers, co-workers, and even from strangers. In order to become successful in life, our youth must learn effective tools for dealing with rejection. One of the main differences between highly successful individuals and those who are less successful is that successful people keep striving to achieve their goals in spite of rejection.

In my university courses and workshop presentations, I often talk about rejection because I consider myself to be an expert on this topic. I've experienced the sting of rejection from relatives, friends, colleagues, church folks, students, and strangers. My decades-long experiences with trying to become a published writer illustrate this fact. I've received hundreds of rejection letters from editors. Each rejection letter disappointed me, and I shed tears over many of them. But in spite of the fact that hundreds of editors rejected my writing projects, I kept praying and writing. After *20 years*, I started to get acceptance letters. If I had let the rejection letters convince me that I couldn't write well or that I would never become a published author, today none of my work would be published because I would've given up long ago. I learned to keep praying and moving towards my goals, even if no one else appeared to believe that I was capable of doing what I set out to do.

Parent-to-Child Rejection. Another lesson that I've learned is that no matter where it comes from, rejection is usually painful. I believe, however, that the ultimate and most painful type of rejection is parent-to-child rejection. For various reasons, countless children have been rejected by one or both parents. Many of these children turn out well in life; others never fully recover from that rejection. Three examples come to mind.

The first example pertains to a woman I met more than 20 years ago. During childhood, she was placed in foster care because her mother was an alcoholic who neglected her children. As the girl was growing up, her mother kept in touch with her and eventually recovered completely from alcoholism. But her daughter never got over the years when she had to live in other people's homes. By the time she became an adult, the rejection she felt as a child had turned into full-fledged anger. I often heard her declare, "I'll never do what my mother did to me! I'll never leave my child the way my mother left me." At the time when she repeatedly told me this, she was married and had a toddler.

As I stated in the previous section, "Actions speak louder than words." Although this woman swore many times that she'd never do what her mother did, she not only eventually abandoned her little girl, but several years later she had another child by another man and abandoned him as well. Because

95

A Brighter Day:
How Parents Can Help African American Youth

she never got over her mother's rejection, she passed this cycle on to two other children. Only time will tell if her two children will follow in her footsteps with their own children.

A second woman I know followed a similar pattern. During her childhood, she felt that her mother put her boyfriends before her. "So, I started acting out in order to get my mother's attention," she said. Even after one of her mother's boyfriends molested her, she continued to believe that she had to compete with men for her mother's attention. After the molestation was revealed, she was placed in foster care, started shoplifting, ended up in juvenile hall, and got hooked on drugs. Later, she had three children by three different men and kept creating situations that required other people to take care of her kids. Each time she got into trouble with the police or social services, quit a job, or got beaten up by one of her "baby daddies," her mother had to rescue her from her latest problem. Clearly the woman was still trying to get something from her mother that she felt she'd never gotten during childhood, and now three innocent children are paying the price for her mother's rejection.

The third example pertains to an African American woman I met several years ago. Although she was in her 50's, she still often cried about her childhood. Her mother was struggling to feed several children, and so when an extended family member offered to help, the mother decided to send the woman away to live with her. The woman couldn't understand why her mother sent *her* away instead of one of her siblings. As a result, she grew up believing that her mother had rejected her. Like the previous two examples, she passed this rejection on to her children. She became an abusive alcoholic. Her own daughter ended up hating her and got

Chapter 4: Seven Life Lessons That Can Empower African American Youth

hooked on drugs, and the daughter's three children ended up in foster care. When I met her, the woman had overcome her alcoholism and was sorry for the abuse that she'd inflicted on her children. However, she said she was too emotionally fragile to raise her grandchildren. When I last spoke with her, her two granddaughters were still living in foster homes, and her grandson had gotten his girlfriend pregnant.

These three stories illustrate how difficult it is for some children to recover from parent-to-child rejection. They also illustrate a point made by Bishop J. W. Walker III, pastor of Mt. Zion Church in Nashville, Tennessee (where my daughter and son-in-law are members). According to Bishop Walker, a victim who does not get help can easily become a victimizer. Because these three women never fully dealt with the rejection they felt from their mothers, each one internalized the rejection, never totally recovered, and passed it on to her own children.

Sibling-Sibling Rejection. Another common type of rejection comes from sibling relationships. Sometimes, older siblings reject younger ones out of the so-called natural sibling rivalry that often occurs in households. I experienced my share of sibling rejection, so I know personally how painful this type of rejection can be. Throughout my entire childhood, one of my sisters hated my guts, and she made no secret of this fact. It wasn't until we became adults that our relationship improved. Then in 1995, after one of our sisters died, we made a vow to become close friends. We kept that promise, and today we are good friends.

Another powerful example of sibling rivalry involves one of my favorite individuals from the Bible. Joseph was hated by his brothers for two main reasons: He was his father's

A Brighter Day:
How Parents Can Help African American Youth

favorite child, and his father didn't hide this fact. He gave
Joseph a special coat, and this made them hate Joseph even
more. Joseph also was a big dreamer. Like many naïve
individuals, he made the mistake of telling the wrong people
about his dreams. When he told his brothers about two of his
dreams, they hated him even more. When their hatred reached
a climax, the brothers decided to kill Joseph but ended up
selling him into slavery instead. They lied to their father and
hid their awful deed. Joseph was heartbroken and suffered
for many years before his dream of becoming a great ruler
came true. When his brothers had to bow down to him and
beg his forgiveness, instead of retaliating, he chose to forgive
them, but he never forgot what they had done.

Of course, not every sibling rejection case has a happy
ending. Some siblings never mend their broken relationships,
and they go to their graves carrying unresolved anger and
pain. Some of the children of David, my second favorite
biblical character, are good examples of this. David, who
became the second king of Israel, had many children, and
some of them didn't get along with each other. One of his
sons, Amnon, raped his half-sister, Tamar. David's son
Absalom retaliated by murdering Amnon and eventually tried
to kill his own father in order to steal his throne. Later, another
son tried to seize the throne from Solomon, and Solomon had
to punish his own brother, whom he couldn't trust. These
sibling-rejection cases didn't have happy endings.

Rejection from Peers. One of the most common types of
rejection is peer rejection. This can start as early as preschool,
when children choose not to play with another child. Of course,
peer rejection can occur at any grade level, and it can also
happen in the neighborhood in which a child grows up. In
order to develop into healthy individuals, all children need

friends. Among other things, interacting with friends helps them improve their social skills, problem-solving skills, and helps them learn how to "manage competition and conflict."[8]

Peer rejection can create lots of problems, including loneliness, depression, and low self-esteem. "Peer rejection is also predictive of later life problems, such as dropping out of school, juvenile delinquency, and mental health problems."[9] Some researchers say that children are more likely to accept other children who are cooperative, fun to be with, loyal, honest, trustworthy, reliable, and who are similar to them in race, gender, and age. Children are more likely to reject peers who are disabled, have "different values and interests," who are aggressive, pushy, dishonest, don't make the peer feel good about himself or herself, and who do not make it easy for the peer to attain his or her goals.[10]

Regardless of the source, rejection can be extremely painful. That's why parents must equip children with strategies to deal with rejection. The following strategies are worth considering:

- Do not condone, tolerate, or foster sibling rivalry.
- Teach children to love and treat their siblings respectfully.
- Teach children how to look for the lessons that they can learn when they are rejected.
- Teach children not to "cast pearls before swine" by reminding them that sometimes the person who is doing the rejecting is not worthy of the child's friendship, loyalty, etc.
- Teach them that rejection can be a blessing in disguise.
- Teach them that rejection can make them emotionally and psychologically stronger if they choose not to let it destroy them.

A Brighter Day:
How Parents Can Help African American Youth

We should teach children that creativity can be a powerful coping tool.

Another important life lesson that we parents should teach our children is how to deal with emotions, such as sadness, anger, and even depression—which according to some researchers is merely anger turned inward. My husband, Rufus, says that when he was growing up, participating in sports gave him a good outlet for anger and negative energy. On the football field, he could be aggressive in ways that he couldn't be off the field. A lot of Black youth get involved in sports, and this gives them something to do with their spare time, teaches them how to follow directions and obey rules, and it also gives them the outlet my husband spoke about.

Not every child will want to participate in sports, so parents should be aware of other healthy emotional outlets. Some children are natural introverts, loners, shy, and deep thinkers. Many of these kids are artistic and extremely creative. Children who are natural artists might automatically turn to music, drawing, painting, writing, etc. whenever they need to express themselves. For instance, my great niece Jayda loves to sing. Singing makes her happy, so she sings in the shower, at bedtime, and whenever she hears a song that she knows. Jayda also makes up her own original songs. Many famous African Americans, such as Kanye West, Donnie McClurkin, Marvin Sapp, Thomas Dorsey, and Quincy Jones, also used music to cope with painful emotions at various times in their lives. In fact, Dorsey wrote the incomparable "Precious Lord" during one of the most tragic periods in his life. Today, decades after he wrote it, this song remains popular during church services and at funerals. Marvin Sapp's "Never Would Have Made It" and McClurkin's "Stand" were also written during challenging periods in their lives.

Chapter 4: Seven Life Lessons That Can Empower African American Youth

During my childhood, I used drawing, painting, and writing to help me deal with painful experiences. In fact, when we were little kids, my younger sister Tammie (who died in 1995) and I spent hours creating our own original paper doll families. We designed beautiful clothes for them, and they became our children. At the time, we were poor Black girls being reared by a single parent in a small apartment in the so-called "ghetto," but when we played with our paper dolls, we created an ideal world for them. Our paper doll families gave us a sense of control that we didn't have in real life, and a way to forget some of the harsh realities that we experienced.

One day, a devastating event occurred. One of my sisters (who hated me at the time) cut off some of my paper dolls' heads. I felt like she'd murdered my babies, and I cried for a long time over their deaths. Even though I eventually created new paper dolls to replace the ones that she'd destroyed, the new ones couldn't replace the ones that I'd lost.

Researchers have found that artistic expression is associated with many positive outcomes, and some therapists even use art therapy to help troubled patients. Art therapy allows patients to express themselves through art or some creative outlet in order to recover from trauma and painful events. Veterans returning from war, children recovering from sexual abuse, and children who have been traumatized by gang violence have all benefited from art therapy.[11] Researchers have concluded that art therapy can also help individuals who are suffering from mental illness, eating disorders, physical illnesses, and other problems.[12]

While some children are naturally inclined to express themselves through artistic outlets, others may not *appear* to be artistic or creative. However, I believe that all children are

A Brighter Day:
How Parents Can Help African American Youth

born with at least one God-given gift or natural talent. We parents can help our children develop healthy creative outlets in several ways:

- Explain to children that artistic expression can be a powerful way to cope with problems.
- Help children uncover their natural gifts and talents by helping them identify what they enjoy doing and what they are good at.
- Make sure that children have access to art supplies at home.
- Expose children to lots of appropriate music by teaching them children's songs, putting them in church and community choirs or chorale groups, giving them music lessons, and encouraging them to join the school band or choir.
- Remember that some quiet, shy, and introverted children may be natural loners who prefer their artistic outlets to people.
- Artists can be extremely sensitive and introverted, so don't tease children, especially boys, who are artistic, and don't allow other people, including siblings and other family members, to tease them either.

Teach them that success is the best revenge.

Many years ago, I heard an African American man tell an interesting story during a Black History Month presentation that he gave at a school where I used to teach. During his childhood, he once had a blatantly racist teacher who often criticized him and told him that he'd never amount to much in life. Soon, he became angry enough to start plotting revenge. Eventually, he decided that success was better than revenge, so he became an overachiever in school. Later, his good grades and hard work enabled him to attend college, where he earned several degrees.

After becoming a professor at a large university, the man returned to his hometown for a visit. He wanted to show the teacher who'd criticized him during childhood that she'd been wrong; he had indeed become successful. However, when he arrived at his old elementary school, he was shocked to learn that the teacher was no longer there; she had died. "I was so mad," he exclaimed, "that I went to the cemetery and stomped on her grave!"

I don't know if this man was joking or serious when he spoke about stomping on his enemy's grave, but I can understand his anger. I'm not proud to admit it, but by nature I'm a vengeful person. The fact that I'm also a sensitive person means that I store up hurts like a miser hoards money. The lessons I learned about hellfire and the law of retribution (payback) in the Pentecostal churches I attended as a child, combined with the personality traits of vengefulness and sensitivity, have been a lethal combination.

However, my motto has become, "Success is the best revenge," and the best way to deal with enemies is to "heap coals of success on their heads." This is the practice I try to live by and one that I tried to instill in my children and my former junior high school and high school students. For example, I once had a high school student who often told me that he hated his stepfather. The stepfather constantly ridiculed him and told him that he was stupid. I urged the student to prove his stepfather wrong by getting good grades in school, making wise choices, and becoming a successful adult.

One of the best examples of the "Success is the best revenge" motto is the story of a man I interviewed for my dissertation research more than 10 years ago. This half-Black,

A Brighter Day:
How Parents Can Help African American Youth

half-White man, whom I'll call "Jermaine," had been very popular during childhood. He was handsome, outgoing, and became a good basketball player. But when he was 12 years old, he suddenly began to lose his hearing. His peers rejected him, and his world "fell apart." According to Jermaine:

> I was a star—the "prima donna" in sports . .
> Everybody wanted to be around me. . .
> Then, when I lost my hearing, quite quickly they just snubbed me. [They] didn't pick me on teams, refused to let me play, couldn't accept losing to me in games. [They] stopped talking to me as if I would spread my deafness to them.[13]

Unfortunately, the rejection didn't just come from kids. Teachers and other adults also started treating him differently. According to Jermaine:

> Teachers stopped calling on me, thinking I had become dumb. Several intentionally embarrassed me in front of the class. Neighbors asked me not to mow their lawns for them anymore [which meant] no more money. Girls openly ridiculed me and gossiped about me. I just became invisible.

As a kid, when I became deaf, all of a sudden I felt I was going to be on my own.

> [I] wasn't going to be able to ask for help or get it. So I had to prepare on my own and not take things lightly. [There was] no room for fun. It was all business. Hearing people only liked me for my athletic skills. The deaf liked me or took to me simply because I was deaf. . . .[14]

Chapter 4: Seven Life Lessons That Can Empower African American Youth

For many years, Jermaine remained bitter about the rejection he experienced. However, he didn't let this bitterness destroy him. After his dream of becoming a college basketball player failed to materialize, he went on to earn a bachelor's degree. He became a teacher at a school for deaf students, and at the time when I interviewed him, he was working on his master's degree. Even though he was still bitter about his experiences, he didn't let them prevent him from becoming successful. This is why his story is worth repeating to youth.

Other simple ways that we can convey the message that "Success is the best revenge" to our children include:

- Tell them explicitly about this message and approach to life.
- Share stories with them about individuals who triumphed over tragedy, rejection, etc. and became successful.
- Explain how they can use their hurts and disappointments to their advantage. Share books with them about this topic. (For adolescents, I recommend Tony Brown's *What Mama Taught Me*, Ben Carson's *The Big Picture*, Antwone Fisher's *Finding Fish*, John Hope Franklin's *Mirror to America*, Tavis Smiley's *What I Know for Sure,* as well as other biographies and autobiographies by African Americans and non-Blacks that emphasize this message.)

Teach children to tithe.

During my childhood, one of the main lessons I learned in all of the tiny Pentecostal churches that I attended was the concept of tithing. Tithing requires that individuals give 10 percent of their increase, salary, etc. to God through the church.

A Brighter Day:
How Parents Can Help African American Youth

The tithe is supposed to be given in addition to a regular monetary offering that is placed in the collection basket.

While I believe that tithing is an important life lesson we should instill in our youth, there is another type of tithing apart from the biblical definition that is also important. This tithing requires that we African Americans give back to the community through our time and effort. Parents should start teaching youth this lesson when they are very young. Giving back to the community means using your gifts and talents to improve social conditions and increase opportunities for inner-city, low-income, and other African Americans who may be wrestling with many of the problems that are common in African American communities throughout the nation.

Lots of famous African Americans have made giving back to the community a top priority in their lives. Oprah Winfrey, for example, has built a school for girls in South Africa, purchased new homes for needy families, donated money to charities, mentored girls, and used her money, influence, and television show to help others. Magic Johnson has used his money and influence to open movie theaters and businesses in Black communities. He has also talked publicly about his struggle with the HIV virus, and he encourages youth to adopt healthy habits. Judge Greg Mathis uses his experiences as an ex-gang member and juvenile delinquent to help youth make better choices than the ones he made. Hydeia Broadbent, who was born with the HIV virus, has co-written a book about the disease, been an AIDs poster child, and tried to increase public awareness about AIDs patients.

Many famous African Americans have helped the Black community, but there are countless other less known African Americans who are also making a positive difference. For

Chapter 4: Seven Life Lessons That Can Empower African American Youth

example, not only has an attorney and friend of mine made her children's education one of her top priorities, she has mentored her nieces and worked with youth at several churches. At one church, she created and taught youth-empowerment classes, and at another, she conducted college preparatory seminars. Another African American attorney friend of mine has given free legal advice to African Americans and has even accompanied several to court—and didn't charge them one cent.

A friend and her husband have started tutoring and college preparatory programs at their church. When an African American woman I know retired from a long career as a social worker in Minnesota, instead of sitting around twiddling her thumbs, she started an advocacy group to help Black children succeed in school. Since then, her organization, which is based in Minneapolis, has partnered with local school districts in an effort to inform teachers and administrators about ways to improve the schooling experiences of African American students.

It's heartwarming for me to know that many African American bishops and pastors have also developed programs to help the Black community. For example, Bishop Charles Blake, the presiding bishop of the Church of God in Christ, has created an Urban Initiative program that is designed to improve many sectors of the Black community. He has also created numerous programs in Africa. Food bank programs, senior citizen homes, education programs, mentoring programs, prison re-entry programs, and financial literacy programs are just a few of the many innovative ministries that African American clergy, such as Bishop Blake, Dr. George McKinney, Bishop Sedgwick Daniels, Bishop Jerry

A Brighter Day:
How Parents Can Help African American Youth

Macklin, Pastor Michael Eaddy, Dr. Terrence Rhone, Dr. Rozario Slack, Bishop J. W. Walker, and others have implemented to empower African Americans.

Parents can teach children the importance of tithing in the form of giving back to the community by simply:

- instilling this message in them when they are young
- teaching them that it's not okay to just make lots of money and have lots of material things
- telling them that true success means making a positive impact on the lives of others
- modeling "giving back to the community" through their actions

Teach them to focus on the Big Picture.

Focusing on the Big Picture—what matters most in life—is a main theme in my own life, and this is an important message that we should teach our children. For me, this message boils down to the simple question, "When I'm on my deathbed and God asks me how I used the gifts, talents, and opportunities that He gave me, will I be proud of the choices I made?" Throughout our lives, we are exposed to many insignificant incidents and problems that can eat away at our time, energy, and effort. So for me, focusing on what really matters in the long run is a good way to stay focused on my main goal in life: to try to live a life that is pleasing to God.

In his book *The Big Picture*, Dr. Ben Carson defines success by how his work affects other people.[15] One of the main reasons why he wrote this book was to share the lessons he learned from challenging circumstances and the principles he lives by with readers. In *What Mama Taught Me: The Seven*

Chapter 4: Seven Life Lessons That Can Empower African American Youth

Core Values of Life, Tony Brown also wrote about the life lessons he learned and the principles by which he lives his life. In the chapter called "The Value of Understanding Your Purpose," Brown urges readers to realize that each of us has God-given talent and potential and that we should "invest our talents" into helping others.[16] This idea forms an important aspect of the Big Picture of his life.

Parents can teach children the importance of focusing on the Big Picture through the following strategies:

- As early as possible, begin teaching children that they have gifts and talents.
- Help them identify their gifts and talents.
- Help them improve their natural gifts and talents.
- Help them identify their long-term goals.
- Help them understand what accomplishing their goals will require.
- Help them figure out the differences between important and unimportant things.
- Help them remember to keep their personal Big Picture foremost in their mind.

A Final Word

There's no way in the world for us to each our children every single thing that they need to know about life before they leave home for good. At best, we should use every opportunity that we can to help our children develop into individuals of whom we will be proud, individuals who make positive contributions to society, individuals who use their gifts and talents wisely, and individuals who will grow up to become outstanding parents themselves. The important lessons that I described in this chapter—teaching youth how

A Brighter Day:
How Parents Can Help African American Youth

to deal with toxic people; teaching youth that it's important to forgive but not forget; that rejection is an unavoidable aspect of life; that creativity can become a powerful coping strategy; that success is the best revenge; that tithing is important; and teaching youth to focus on the Big Picture—are only seven of the many life tools that I believe that we should equip our children with before they leave home.

Chapter 5

How Can We Help Our Children Succeed at School?

One of the main reasons why I wrote this book was to counter the stereotype that African Americans aren't good parents. A related stereotype is that most of us don't care about our children's education. When I conduct workshops for educators throughout the nation, this is one of the main stereotypes that I address. This stereotype is difficult for me to combat because many school principals and teachers are thoroughly convinced that we don't care about our children's education. Even when I tell them about research that shows that most African American parents do care about their children's education, many remain skeptical, and some of the main skeptics happen to be Black educators!

There are many reasons why this belief is so common, and the black-white achievement gap is at the top of the list. This simply means that Black K–12 students tend to have lower standardized test scores than most White students at the same grade levels. In recent years, other gaps have emerged, indicating that Black students' test scores are lower, on average, than the scores of many Latino and Asian American students as well. Many educators blame parents for these low test scores.

Another reason why many educators don't believe that most of us care about our children's education is because they assume that we aren't actively involved in helping our children succeed academically. When we fail to show up for Back to School Night and Open House, when our kids don't turn in

A Brighter Day:
How Parents Can Help African American Youth

their homework and repeatedly earn low grades, or when they miss a lot of school, many educators assume it's our fault.

Furthermore, Black children are more likely than any other group to be suspended and expelled from school. Even though research has shown that the school system often engages in racist and unfair discipline policies and practices,[1] the fact that our children are more likely to get into trouble at school causes educators to conclude that our youth come from bad homes. In other words, if we raised them properly and cared about their education, our kids would behave at school.

There is clearly a difference between reality and perception: Educators believe that we don't care about our children's education, yet research has shown that most of us do.[2] Nevertheless, since it's in our children's best interest, we should work as closely as possible with educators. According to the National PTA/Building Successful Partnerships initiative, the benefits of parent involvement include higher grades and test scores, better attendance, and increased high school graduation rates and college enrollment.[3]

Obviously being highly involved in our children's education will benefit our youth. But during my travels throughout the United States, I often meet African American parents, and sometimes even White and Latino parents of half-Black children, who say they are concerned about their children's education and that they need help. Many of these parents have shared some very sad stories with me. Other parents have emailed me or telephoned me to discuss their children's education. Most are crying out for information that will enable them to do a better job of helping their children succeed at school. Therefore, in this chapter, I share stories and strategies that parents can use to help our youth succeed academically.

Chapter 5: How Can We Help Our Children Succeed at School

We must set the right tone about education when our children are young.

Too often, we parents knowingly or unknowingly set a tone in our homes that sends a negative message about priorities. Because children learn by example, it's not enough for us to *say* that we value education; we must also *show* it through our actions, what we encourage children to do, and how we encourage them to spend their time.

For example, one little African American boy was taught early in life that basketball is important. When he was just a toddler, his teenage uncles taught him how to dribble and shoot a ball. By the time he was three or four, basketball had become his favorite hobby and he seemed to never tire of throwing, dribbling, and shooting the ball. Shortly after he started elementary school, teachers complained to his mother that he wouldn't sit still in class. As he grew older, teachers complained that he had a short attention span and didn't like to read. His mom, a single parent, was strict about making him do his homework. She kept in touch with his teachers on a regular basis and took their concerns seriously. But no matter how hard she tried, she kept hearing complaints about her son's behavior at school. By second grade, the child hated reading and doing his homework, yet this same child could sit still, focus intently, and master video games. In fact, when he was playing video games, he seemed to be in a different world. He could tune out all distractions, and he acted like nothing else mattered but the game that he was playing at the moment.

In many of his books, Dr. Jawanza Kunjufu offers practical suggestions to parents about how we can create a culture of learning in the home. In *Developing Positive Self-Images &*

A Brighter Day:
How Parents Can Help African American Youth

Discipline in Black Children, he encourages parents to set a positive tone in the home in the following ways:
- Have a structured schedule in the home.
- Ask children to explain what they did at school.
- Ensure that children use their time at home wisely.
- Restrict and monitor television viewing.
- Make sure children receive proper nutrition.
- Play educational games with children.[4]

If children have already developed bad habits (e.g., watching too much television and spending too much time playing video games), parents should turn the situation around as soon as possible.

We must surround our children with people who value education.

Because the people with whom our children associate have either a positive or a negative impact on them, it's important for us to surround them with individuals who have the same values we have. This is especially true when it comes to education. So many of us try to teach our children that education is important, only to realize that our goals have been undermined by people with different values. Often these people are the children's peers or even extended family members who promote anti-education messages.

Kunjufu, Comer, and Poussaint have written extensively about how various individuals in the Black community plant anti-education messages in the minds of Black youth and how powerful the peer group can be. This is why it's important for us to know our children's friends, and why we should be vigilant about helping our youth select the right friends and associates. So many of us think that as long as we're *telling* our children to do the right thing, our children will turn out

Chapter 5: How Can We Help Our Children Succeed at School

well even if they associate with relatives and friends who don't share our values. However, this is a very dangerous and naïve assumption.

I've seen several cases where Black mothers tried to teach their sons to go to school, get good grades, etc. while allowing certain negative individuals—uncles, cousins, and others—to have contact with their sons. The boys ended up rejecting the mothers' value systems and following the negative male role models.

One of my sisters, a single parent, was a brilliant high achiever who valued education, but her son chose to follow in his uncle's path instead of hers. When he was four years old, her son started saying, "I want to be just like Uncle Calvin." At the time, Calvin was a drug addict and a gang member who believed that Black people who went to college were just trying to "act White." Even though my sister worked hard and earned two college degrees before she died in 1995, her son did exactly what he said he was going to do: He followed in Uncle Calvin's footsteps instead of his mother's.

Extended family members and others may ridicule and criticize us for not letting our children associate with "bad influences," but I'm convinced that this is absolutely necessary. We *must* surround our children with people who share our values and who promote positive messages about education.

We must not give our children mixed messages about education.

Some African Americans who *say* they value education send mixed messages to our children. Although education historically has been highly valued in the Black community, some Black folks continue to have a love-hate relationship

A Brighter Day:
How Parents Can Help African American Youth

with educated African Americans. On the one hand, they are proud of our accomplishments, but on the other hand, jealousy often surfaces. It is necessary for parents to send one message to children: "Education is important!" We shouldn't allow jealousy and insecurity to make us *say* that we value education while *acting* like we don't. For example:

- We shouldn't accuse educated Blacks of acting White.
- We shouldn't make fun of African Americans who speak Standard English.
- We shouldn't allow our children to tease, ridicule, or bully high-achieving African American children.
- We shouldn't teach our children that it's not "cool" to be smart.[5]

We must know how to deal with educators.

Of course, in order to be successful advocates for our children, we must know how to deal effectively with K–12 educators. This requires knowing what teachers think about our children, our culture, us as parents, etc. and doing our best to prevent potential problems. Two of the main ways that we can decrease the chances of our children having problems with teachers relate to behavior and appearance.

Our children should arrive at school looking clean, well groomed, well fed, and wearing age-appropriate clothing. Girls shouldn't wear skin-tight clothing, revealing clothing, clothing that shows the belly, or skirts, dresses, and tops that are too short. Boys shouldn't wear gang attire or pants that are so baggy that the underwear shows. When we give into the pressure of allowing our children to wear any and everything to school just because it's the latest fad, we're asking for trouble and may be setting our children up for failure. It's important for us to remember that many teachers—Blacks and non-Blacks—are quick to stereotype our children based on how they dress.

In addition to being dressed appropriately, our children should arrive at school with supplies and materials: lined paper, pencils, homework, etc. Furthermore, we must do our best to make sure that our children *act* the way they're supposed to act in school. It is true that unfair school policies and cultural misunderstandings play a large role in promoting the common belief among educators that Black students cause the most problems in class. However, it is also true that some African American students *do* misbehave in school, and they do need to suffer the consequences of their actions. It is difficult (though not impossible) for educators to teach children who are exposed to inappropriate behaviors at home, have poor role models, and aren't disciplined properly. When we lose control of our children, we shouldn't be surprised when teachers say our children have behavioral problems. The following suggestions can prevent many problems for our children at school:

- Teach children to treat adults and other children respectfully.
- Teach children the difference between an "inside" voice and an "outside" voice. An inside voice should be used inside the classroom and other buildings. It has a lower tone than an outside voice, and it should only be heard by those to whom the child is speaking. An outside voice is louder, one that children can use when they are on the playground or interacting with family and friends away from school, in the privacy of their own home, etc. Tell children to lower their voice when they are speaking too loudly, and teach them when it's okay to use the outside versus inside

voice. Compliment them when they use the inside voice at appropriate times, and model to them in stores and other public places how to use an inside voice.

- Teach children not to talk back to teachers, school administrators, or authority figures, even when the authority figure appears to be wrong. When a child is treated unfairly, he should know (based on what you've taught him) to tell you what happened and let you handle it from there. Arrange to meet with the teacher, administrator, or staff member to discuss the problem.

- Teach children how to use their time wisely when they finish their class work early. After checking over her work, the child can ask the teacher for an extra credit assignment, read a book or appropriate magazine, or get a head start on another assignment, such as reading the next section of the textbook, etc.

- Tell your child not to sleep in class, not to talk to other students during class time without permission, not to pass notes, and to remain seated unless the teacher has given the student permission to stand up. Having too much idle time is one of the main reasons why African American children get into trouble at school. They use this time to engage in behaviors that teachers view as disruptive.

- Never ever condone inappropriate behavior. If a child has been punished at school for misbehaving, the parent should support the teacher, discipline the child in an appropriate way, and insist that the child apologizes to the teacher. One of the worse things we can do is to side with a child who is guilty. This is a great way to help children become career criminals.

Chapter 5: How Can We Help Our Children Succeed at School

- Those of us who have already lost control of a child and can't get the child to behave properly at home need to seek professional help, preferably from a licensed African American therapist, as soon as possible. Those of us who can't control our own children shouldn't criticize teachers and school administrators when the child's negative school "rap sheet" starts to grow. It is extremely irresponsible for us to allow this pattern of misbehavior to continue without taking drastic action.

We must know how to work effectively with teachers and administrators.

We should also equip ourselves with some basic strategies to deal effectively with teachers and school administrators. First and foremost, we should remember that just as stereotypes are common about our children, many K–12 educators believe negative stereotypes about parents as well. I've already stated that most educators don't believe that we are good parents, and most don't believe that we care about our children's education.

A third stereotype is that our homes are chaotic, unstructured, and unclean. For example, an African American educator in Minnesota told me that she takes teachers to visit the homes of struggling students. Just a few days before she attended my presentation, she had taken a White teacher to visit the home of an African American student who was earning poor grades. When they left the home, the White teacher said she was amazed at how clean and organized the home was and how well the child's mother could multi-task. While conferring with the teacher, the mother had been making tacos while her son was doing his homework at the kitchen table. The educator who told me this story was disgusted by the teacher's reaction; apparently, the teacher had walked into that home with a head full of stereotypes about African American families.

Another common stereotype is that many educators view African American parents as being hostile, aggressive, and unpleasant to deal with. Many would prefer to have as little contact with us as possible. Sometimes, righteous indignation and anger are completely justified. Nevertheless, there are a few basic points that we should keep in mind when dealing with school administrators and teachers. These points can be organized under the biblical scripture that says "Be angry but sin not." In other words, even when you are justifiably angry, keep the following "Do's and Don'ts" in mind:

- Always be polite and respectful.
- Plan what you're going to say ahead of time by writing down the main concerns you would like to have addressed and the outcomes you would like to occur.
- Be persistent and unwavering in serving as an advocate for your children.
- Do not use put downs, profanity, insults, or a condescending tone or language.
- Do not point your finger, roll your eyes, yell, put your hands on your hips, roll your neck, or engage in behaviors that are viewed as combative, hostile, or threatening.
- Do not let educators' degrees, credentials, level of education, or big words intimidate you or make you feel dumb or inferior.
- Do not be embarrassed or ashamed to ask educators to repeat, re-explain, or give examples to clarify statements.

Chapter 5: How Can We Help Our Children Succeed at School

- Keep a paper trail consisting of names, dates, and descriptions of all meetings and telephone conferences with school personnel.
- Put your concerns in writing, and keep copies of any letters, notes, etc. that you send to school personnel.
- Contact the "big guns"—school board members, the school superintendent, local politicians, the state board of education, community leaders, and even the media—if your concerns are repeatedly ignored.
- Be aware that some teachers may retaliate against your child if you have complained. In this case, document everything and contact the "big guns."

The final point that I'll make about parent-teacher and parent-administrator interaction is that we should remember that many teachers and administrators do care about the academic welfare of our children, and many try to be fair to them. Educators who have high expectations aren't the enemy and aren't picking on our kids. I was reminded of this point as I was writing this book. At the end of one of my presentations, a young African American elementary school principal in Georgia described some of her experiences to me.

This woman loved her job, loved her students, tried to compel teachers to give students an outstanding education, and believed that God had placed her in a position to serve as an advocate for Black children. But her biggest problem was the parents—particularly African American parents. On numerous occasions, Black parents had treated her disrespectfully, ignored her advice, and set their children up for failure at school. "If we could just get our Black parents to understand that they are doing their kids a disservice when they don't allow us to put the supports in place for them," she said, "lots of problems could be avoided."

In one case, she had repeatedly told the mother and grandmother of an African American student that he was headed in the wrong direction and needed remediation. Although they weren't as rude as some other Black parents had been, they ignored her advice and didn't allow the child to receive the intervention he needed. At the end of his fourth grade year, they were distraught to learn that the child would not be promoted to fifth grade because he couldn't read.

The main point the principal wanted me to share with African American parents is that "I love the kids. You've had your chance. Now give your child a running start in order to compete in life." This story should remind us that many educators do have our children's best interests at heart, which is why it is so important that we form positive relationships with these educators.

We must help our children develop good reading skills.

Each year, countless K–12 students are passed through the system with poor reading skills. Black students tend to be over represented among the students who read below grade level, and on standardized tests, Black students are more likely to have lower reading scores than most of their non-Black grade-level peers. Because reading is so important and it's easy for African American K–12 students to be passed along year after year with poor reading skills, parents shouldn't depend on the school system to teach children how to read, read well, and develop a love for reading.

The following strategies that I used with my great niece Jayda and my own three children can help parents improve children's reading skills:

Chapter 5: How Can We Help Our Children Succeed at School

- Buy books for children, and take your child to the public library to check out books on a regular basis.
- Encourage children to check out books from the school library or classroom library on a regular basis.
- Read to children daily.
- Ask children to read to you on a regular basis. This can take place while you're cooking dinner, doing the laundry, or performing some other household chore.
- Encourage children to read to their younger brothers and sisters.
- Make sure that children understand the reading material by having them tell you what the story is about.
- If a child does not know a word, ask him/her to look it up in a dictionary and write the meaning on an index card. The child can keep a box of index cards of new words and review them periodically.
- Model reading to children by letting them see you read books and magazines for pleasure.
- Remember that books are valuable gifts for birthdays and holidays.
- Make sure that your child is getting homework several nights a week.
- Check your child's homework.
- If you can't help him with the work, ask the teacher or principal to assign a peer tutor to help your child.

We must help our children develop good math skills.
Many African American high school students lack the math skills they need to perform increasingly complicated math functions. Furthermore, children are expected to do

higher-level math at much younger ages than we were. That's why so many of us have difficulty helping our children, even with elementary school math.

Students who start on a downward math path in elementary school often drop out of school by ninth or tenth grade. Because math skills (especially algebra) are so crucial to students' academic success, I recommend that parents use the following strategies:

- When children are very young, teach them how to count.
- As children get older, teach them how to add, subtract, count money, and tell time.
- Purchase flashcards, math games, and math workbooks from stores and bookstores to help children learn.
- Those of us who have weak math skills can improve them by using elementary-level math workbooks and then higher-level math books. This should help us help our children.
- By the time students are required to do algebra, they should know the order of operations: parentheses, exponents, multiply, divide, add, and subtract. Make sure children know how to *do e*ach operation. Children who don't know how to multiply or divide will have trouble doing algebraic equations correctly.
- Make sure that children learn all the rules for adding, subtracting, multiplying, and dividing numbers that have positive or negative signs.
- Make sure that children have high enough math grades to qualify them for college-preparatory high school math courses.

Chapter 5: How Can We Help Our Children Succeed at School

- Learn the difference between college-preparatory high school math courses and non-college preparatory courses.
- During summer, winter, and spring breaks, insist that children spend time daily reading for recreational purposes and improving their math skills.

We must help our children develop a college-going mindset.

During a workshop that I conducted at an elementary school in Watts, an African American teacher disagreed with my comment that teachers should start to develop a college-going mindset in students as early as elementary school. Although I shared some examples of how teachers could do this, told them the reasons why I thought it was important, and also described several elementary school teachers who were already doing this, the young Black teacher still disagreed with my position. She said, "I tell my students that college isn't for everyone. There's nothing wrong with being a plumber, and if they want to be a plumber, they should become the best plumber they can be." Of course, she was correct. There's nothing wrong with being a plumber. Every home and apartment needs a good plumbing system, and when there's a plumbing problem, a good plumber is what the homeowner needs. So, there is nothing wrong with a person *choosing* to become a plumber when he or she grows up. In fact, one of my African American acquaintances, an attorney and author who has several college degrees, married her plumber.

The problem that I have is that some teachers give African American children the impression that jobs that don't require a college education are the *only* employment options available to them. I also have a problem with teachers and school counselors who force our youth to take non-college preparatory classes because they don't think that our kids are smart enough, capable enough, or deserving enough to attend college.

Later, that same African American teacher came up to me and explained why she felt as she did. It turned out that she had actually grown up in Watts and had been a high achiever during her schooling. She graduated from high school early, got admitted to a prestigious local, private university, and would ride several buses to attend the university. Unfortunately, she felt lonely and out of place. So, she eventually dropped out of college, and it took many years for her to develop the confidence to return to college and earn a degree and a teaching credential. Because her own personal experience had been painful, she wanted to spare her students from a similar fate by convincing them that "college wasn't for everyone."

I agree that college isn't necessarily for everyone, that some well paying jobs don't require a college degree, and that there's nothing wrong with having a job that doesn't require one. However, I strongly believe that every K–12 student should have the *choice* and the *option* to attend college and that educators shouldn't make this decision for them. I also believe that every teacher and every African American parent should try to instill a college-going mindset in children. Then, we should let the children ultimately decide on their career path when they are old enough to make a wise decision. A lot of people, such as the aforementioned African American teacher, disagree with me, but I feel very strongly about this point. There are five main reasons why I believe this.

Chapter 5: How Can We Help Our Children Succeed at School

Earning a college degree is one of the best ways for African Americans to increase their chances of earning higher incomes. Many of the highest paying professions, such as medicine and law, require college degrees, and the average college graduate earns more money than individuals who only have a high school diploma, a GED, or less education.[6] Today, many high paying jobs in the United States are being taken by college-educated adults from other countries because so many American-born citizens don't have the strong math and science backgrounds that are needed.

African Americans are more likely to live at or below the poverty level than any other group.[7] In some families, poverty and high unemployment have become generational cycles. In others, generational cycles were broken because a Black parent chose to encourage her children to attend college. My grandmother, Francis, and her husband, Leonard, are two good examples of this. Although my grandmother had to quit school and clean White people's homes, she and her husband, my step grandfather, taught the children who were raised under their roof that education is important. They expected them to do well in school and attend college. Two daughters went to nursing school, one daughter became a teacher, another daughter became a business woman, and the son became a fire fighter.

Although my grandmother grew up in a shack with no running water in East Texas and was unable to complete her K–12 schooling, she made sure that her children would have a better future by teaching them that education could improve their lives. And it did. Most of the children who were raised under my grandmother's roof passed the legacy that their parents started onto their children. Many of my grandmother's grandchildren went to college, and now several of her great

A Brighter Day:
How Parents Can Help African American Youth

grandchildren are doing the same thing. What could have become a generational cycle of poverty was broken by the "education is important" mindset that my grandmother and her husband instilled in their children.

Individuals should be able to take care of themselves financially. Every adult should be self-supporting and self-sufficient. It is dangerous for adults to have to depend on other people for food, clothing, transportation, and shelter. An African American woman I met after one of my presentations learned this the hard way. She married a wealthy African American man who owned his own airplane and several fabulous homes. He flew her around the world and bought her expensive clothes—but there was a price tag attached to his generosity. He wanted to control her every move, and over time, his controlling behavior increased. She soon realized that the man was "a nut case." When she eventually escaped from that marriage, she had to leave behind all of the fine material possessions he had given her. However, because she had already earned a college degree and a teaching credential before she married him, after the divorce she was quickly able to find a teaching job. When I met her, she was still recovering emotionally from that marriage, but she was thankful that she could now decide where she could and couldn't go, what she could and couldn't wear, and when and what to eat. More important, she was happy that *she* could support herself financially, thanks to her college education.

The old saying, "Knowledge is power," is true indeed. When we know our rights and how to find the information and resources that we need, we are in a better position to protect ourselves and help others. One of the best examples is the late Johnny Cochran, the famous African American attorney who represented O.J. Simpson.

Chapter 5: How Can We Help Our Children Succeed at School

Cochran graduated from law school and began to work in the Los Angeles District Attorney's Office because he believed in America's judicial system. Over time, he realized that the system is racist, corrupt, and unfair, so he decided to become a criminal and civil attorney in order to help the very people who were being mistreated by the justice system. He used his education, position, and influence to become a strong advocate for African Americans and to teach people how to fight for their rights.[8]

The late Dr. John Hope Franklin is another example of an African American who used his knowledge to educate others and to fight the system. Franklin, who became a famous historian and author of numerous books, got tired of the anti-Black lies that White historians were spreading, including the lie that the slaves didn't suffer much and weren't unhappy about slavery. In addition to collaborating on a textbook for school children that showed the many ways in which African Americans have contributed to society, Franklin wrote numerous history books in order to dispel myths and outright lies about African Americans. He also did a lot of the background work that led to the Brown versus Board of Education case, and even though he died in 2009 while in his 90s, he continued to use his education to openly fight racism until the end of his life. In his excellent autobiography, he did a wonderful job of explaining how institutional racism has destroyed countless African American males. One of these victims was his older brother, a school principal who was eventually destroyed by racism.[9]

The fifth reason why I believe that parents should instill a college-going mindset in children early in life is personal: Earning multiple college degrees has truly improved the quality of my life. During part of my childhood, my family

A Brighter Day:
How Parents Can Help African American Youth

was on welfare, but we ended up joining the ranks of the working class after my mother got a decent paying job. Years later, when I became a struggling single parent, I was able to join the middle class because my prayers and my bachelor's degree opened the door for me to join the K–12 teaching force. This allowed me to secure medical benefits for my daughter and me. My husband, Rufus, who also grew up on welfare, earned two college degrees, and like my grandmother Francis, we made it clear to our children that we wanted them to use education to improve their lives. My oldest daughter, Nafissa, and her husband, Derrick, are doctoral students at a prestigious university. My second daughter, NaChe', is a college undergraduate, and my son, Stephen, is a college sophomore. We also told my great niece Jayda that we wanted her to go to college one day. We took her to college events and told her why attending college is important.

Finally, we should instill a college-going mindset in our children early because many of them are interested in pursuing jobs that require a college education. For example, many African American children dream of becoming doctors or lawyers when they grow up. However, they might not have any idea of how to make those dreams a reality. If their parents never attended college, they may not know how to help their children attain their dreams. The following simple strategies can be helpful to our children:

- When children are young, start explaining what college is and why attending is important.
- Take children to visit local colleges and universities.
- Expose children to college-educated African Americans who are down-to-earth.
- Enroll children in college-preparatory and summer enrichment programs.

Chapter 5: How Can We Help Our Children Succeed at School

- Make sure that children are placed in college preparatory middle school and high school classes.
- Make sure that children take the required number of courses and the correct math, English, and science courses that are necessary for college admission.
- Help children learn how to navigate the college admissions process. Find out about application deadlines, how to get applications, how to apply for financial aid, etc.
- Use the Internet, bookstores, college graduates, and school counselors as resources.
- Make sure that children have strong reading, writing, and math skills long before they graduate from high school.

A Final Word: We should encourage our children to use their education to help themselves and the community.

In the late 1970s when I returned home after my first year of college, I noticed an interesting pattern. Some friends and family members automatically assumed that I would act "stuck up." In other words, they assumed that one year of college would go to my head, and I would act like I was better than others. This same pattern occurred after my first book was published. In each of these situations, I had to work hard to let these individuals know that I hadn't changed. I was the same ole Gail.

Years later, two events helped me to understand why this pattern occurred. The first was an interview that I conducted for one of my book projects. An African American parent told me that during his childhood, he had attended all-Black, segregated, K–12 schools in the South, and he resented the way that some of the Black teachers had treated him. These teachers showed favoritism towards light-skinned children and children who came from higher-income families, he said. When I mentioned this to one of my African American graduate students, a woman who had attended segregated schools in Florida, she said these practices were common in her schools, but she still believed that the teachers in the segregated schools were much better than many teachers today because most instilled a sense of pride in the educational achievements of their students.

The second incident occurred when I was in an airport one day, waiting to catch a plane for a workshop that I'd been invited to conduct. I'd been talking casually to three elderly Black women who were also waiting to board the same plane. The conversation went smoothly until they learned that I was an educator. All of a sudden, they looked at me coldly, and one said, "I grew up in the South where Black teachers thought they were better than other people." Then, without uttering another word to me, the women moved away from me, as if I had a contagious disease.

Since then, I've heard similar stories from others about past and recent events. An African American high school principal in Los Angeles said he knows of cases where Black teachers tell Black students, "Your mama ain't nothing, and you'll never amount to anything either." Some Black teachers have even told principals that they prefer not to work with African American students. Teachers like this give Black teachers a bad reputation.

Nevertheless, I strongly believe that education is important, that we need to use education to help ourselves and the community, and that education has always been valued by Black people, even though some of us have spread mixed

Chapter 5: How Can We Help Our Children Succeed at School

messages about it and some of us have used our education as a way of putting others down to make ourselves appear to be superior. I also believe that we should be actively involved in our children's education and that we should encourage our children to attend college.

However, it's important for us to teach our children that in spite of their education, they will still encounter racism, for no amount of education in the world will prevent certain individuals from believing that we deserve less, are not worthy of respect, are not intelligent, etc. My bachelor's degree, teaching credential, master's degree, and doctorate have not prevented me from experiencing racism, and it would be foolish of me not to prepare my children for this reality. Nevertheless, I am still proud of my educational accomplishments and proud that my own children are following in my footsteps. Even if some people are too narrow-minded, too ignorant, too jealous, or too racist to value the degrees I have worked hard to earn, what I've accomplished is something that can never be taken away from me. I am not wealthy, but my education has qualified me for high-paying jobs that would have been off limits without my degrees. I was reminded of this very point recently as I read an article in *Ebony* magazine.

In "The Pursuit of Life After Prison," author Shirley Henderson described several former African American inmates who turned their lives around. Two of these individuals made thousands of dollars per week selling drugs before they were eventually arrested.[10] In his autobiography, Judge Greg Mathis described a former friend who became a big drug dealer. This man often made fun of Mathis after Mathis decided to use education as a legitimate route to improve his life. In the end, Mathis had the last laugh because his friend was eventually forced to pay for his choices. The educational investment Mathis made in himself opened up many legitimate opportunities, including his popular television show.[11]

These stories and others like them should remind us that a good education is something that no one can ever take away from us or our children, and stories like these are worth sharing with youth who might be thinking about taking the fast route to riches.

Chapter 6

Preparing Our Youth for the Workforce

One day, more than 20 years ago, I was in the bank with my toddler daughter when an African American bank teller gave me some important advice: "Don't make the mistake that I made with my child," she warned. "I gave my son everything he wanted. Now he's a grown man who won't get a job and expects to live off of me." Because I've always tried to learn from other people's mistakes, I took the woman's advice to heart. Therefore, as my three children were growing up, I tried to teach them the importance of working for what they want in life.

Later, one of the main lessons that I learned from my dissertation research was that the successful African Americans whom I interviewed and the college students who participated in the study all had a strong work ethic when they were growing up. These individuals grew up believing that achieving their goals required hard work and that their hard work would eventually pay off. My own personal experiences and the lessons I've learned from successful (and less successful) individuals have convinced me that instilling a strong work ethic in our children is one of the greatest gifts that we can give to them. In this chapter, I share stories and strategies regarding the importance of teaching our youth that hard work pays off, and I also explain how we can prepare them for the workforce.

The Benefits of Hard Work

Too often, those of us who grew up in poverty try to overcompensate by giving our children too much. We waste

A Brighter Day:
How Parents Can Help African American Youth

money on expensive clothing, designer sneakers, and other things that our children don't need in order to impress or compete with other people. As a result, some children become extremely materialistic, and their priorities are not in order.

A second common problem, especially in inner city neighborhoods plagued by high unemployment, is that many youth and adults resort to selling drugs in order to make money quickly. One of my brothers fell into this trap and got locked into a vicious cycle that he was still trying to escape when he died. A similar story involves another African American man who became a notorious drug pusher. I met him when I went to Minnesota several years ago to give a presentation. Unlike my brother who dealt drugs as a teenager, used drugs shortly thereafter, and ended up dying in prison at age 42, this man's story had a happy and unusual ending.

At the time when I met him, the man was a grandfather who had been through "hell and high water." He never knew his biological parents but had been adopted by a middle-class African American couple who gave him and his adopted sister a good life. But they also gave him too much. "I didn't want everything handed to me," he said. "I wanted to do it myself."

As he grew older, his curiosity about his biological parents increased. He had assumed that they'd been poor and had given him up for adoption so that he could have a better life, but what he learned shocked him and propelled him down a self-destructive path that could have destroyed him. He found out that his biological parents actually had college degrees and several other children. However, he was the only child that they gave up for adoption. Consequently, he felt rejected, and that something had to be wrong with him.

When he was 11 or 12 years old, he started smoking marijuana, and by age 16 or 17, he was selling drugs and carrying guns to protect himself and the large sums of drug money that he carried. Drug dealing "was the easiest way [to make money]," he told me, "and I had connections to get [drugs] and not have to spend a lot of money. It was very lucrative. It's sad to look at it that way, but that's just how it was." Although he was making a lot of money, as he grew older, his need to *use* his merchandise also increased. At age 18, he was "smoking, drinking, and shooting" drugs constantly. He got married, bought a big house in the suburbs, drove fancy cars, and had several children. Suburbia was a perfect place for him to live and work since "They got more drugs in the suburbs than they do in the inner city because that's where all the money is. But they get it on the DL [down low]."

Money or no money, fancy cars or not, this lifestyle was dangerous. "People were shooting at me with guns that went through the cars, Mac 10s and AK 47s," he explained. "My family could've been killed." Over time, as his and his wife's drug habits increased, they started to lose everything they owned, and he soon became homeless. "I smoked everything up, used it all up doing the drugs," he said. For three years, from ages 25 to 28, he was homeless. Furthermore, his entire extended family got tired of being taken advantage of by him, and eventually turned against him.

After 12 or 13 years of being addicted to drugs and going through three-court ordered drug treatment programs, the turning point came when he was sent to an African American-run treatment center in the Twin Cities. He was successful the fourth time because his counselor used effective techniques. Today, this former drug pusher has not only been reunited with his family and been forgiven by them, but he is also a successful business owner who owns two houses that he got *legally* and by working hard. He is also trying to make amends for the damage that he did to society during his years as a drug pusher and drug addict. "I've been given a second chance. . . and it's something that I don't want to mess up," he explained. "I believe that my Higher Power was there looking over me because I was shot, stabbed, and survived it all."

Now, he not only tries to be a good role model to his adult children and his grandchildren, but he also mentors juveniles who have been sent to reform school. He said that many of these youth have no fear of being sent to prison "because the home lives that they come from are just as difficult as the prison. A lot of them have been beaten. . . . A lot of them have to supply their mother's and father's or mom's boyfriend's drug habit. Now that's a devastating blow!" Because he has walked in their shoes, he finds that many of the youth, especially young Black males, are willing to listen to what he has to share. He explained:

> I want to try to correct the wrongs that I've done in my past to try to make the future a little better for somebody else, the children. It's gonna take a lot for all of us to help the children. [The work] is not a lot, but it's something that I can give back. There's not a lot of White kids in there [reform school and juvenile hall].
>
> I tell them my story and they have a hard time believing it, but I was there, and I can identify with anybody who is there. But I have to disassociate myself from them. . . . I still believe that I am chemically dependent. I'm too weak to associate with people who are doing drugs. I don't go to bars.

Chapter 6: Preparing Our Youth for the Workforce

This story illustrates a point that I've often told my children and great niece Jayda: "There are two ways to learn things in life: the easy way and the hard way." The man who shared his story with me learned the hard way that it's best to use legal channels to improve one's life.

In my own life, I've seen how a strong work ethic can pay off. During my childhood, I learned that reaching my goals would require hard work. My mother was instrumental in teaching me this lesson. When most of my siblings and I were little kids, she made us do chores on a regular basis. Sometimes, it seemed that on Saturdays, we cleaned almost all day long. When I turned seven, my mother added cleaning the kitchen to my regular list of chores, and as I grew older, she expected more from me. I also started babysitting for neighbors when I was still in elementary school as a way to earn extra money, and when I was in junior high school, for a short time, I worked as a live-in caretaker of a woman who'd had a stroke. After that, I worked as the church receptionist, which basically required me to answer the telephone each day after school. Next, I spent two summers working as a file clerk for the Social Security Administration. The following summer, I worked as a bookkeeper at a bank. During the school term, I worked as a housekeeper, sweeping, mopping, dusting, washing dishes, vacuuming, and doing other chores at the home of an administrator of the high school I attended. In later years, I worked as a waitress, member of a summer dormitory-cleaning crew, a tutor, receptionist, summer intern reporter for a newspaper, Peace Corps Volunteer, substitute teacher, full-time teacher, university professor, workshop presenter, and consultant. With the exception of the newspaper internship, the Peace Corps job, and the university professorship, If I'd had my choice, I wouldn't have chosen

A Brighter Day:
How Parents Can Help African American Youth

several of these jobs. On the surface, they didn't appear to lead to my overall goal of becoming a news reporter and book author. The road that led to my dreams wasn't smooth, and I often had to take the jobs that were available at the time. Today, however, I've attained my dream of becoming a book author, and I can honestly say that all of my previous jobs gave me rich experiences and taught me important lessons that I use in my writing, teaching, and workshop presentations. In other words, my hard work really has paid off.

The following strategies can help us instill in our children the message that "hard work pays off":

- Require all members of the household to do chores, and be fair about assigning chores.
- Encourage children to do extra chores to earn money for special items they want.
- Teach children that they shouldn't expect to start at the top, but be willing to accept other jobs when necessary as they pursue their goals.
- Teach children that the world doesn't owe them anything, and they shouldn't expect to be given things for which they haven't worked.
- Teach children to dream big, but also understand that the road to attaining their dreams will require hard work, sacrifice, and persistence.
- Do not give children too many material things.
- Share books and stories with children about individuals who used hard work to improve their lives.

Preparing Youth for the Workforce

One day when I was a college sophomore, I heard the words that no employee ever wants to hear: "You're fired!" Today, nearly 30 years from that fateful day, I can still remember the shame that overwhelmed me when that thunderbolt struck. Even though I hated my job and couldn't stand my new boss, I never wanted—nor expected—to be fired. But the boss had fired me, and I immediately felt ashamed and fearful. I was ashamed because even though I'd been working since elementary school, I'd never been fired before. I was fearful because I needed that job in order to stay in school. I had already lost one of my tuition scholarships, and this job was helping me to remain at the prestigious university that I attended.

Despite my shock, embarrassment, and terror, deep down inside I knew I deserved to be fired. Almost from the moment the new boss—an Asian-American woman who was just a few years older than me—arrived, I had sized her up and concluded that I didn't like her. Whereas my previous boss, an older White woman, had been kind, caring, and interested in my education, early on the new boss made it clear that she viewed me as a mere "work-study" student who was there to do whatever *she* wanted me to do whenever *she* wanted me to do it. My previous boss had always been careful to make sure that she only asked me to do what I'd been hired to do: file, type, and answer telephones. But the new boss expected me to do things that weren't in my job description. Therefore, each time she summoned me into her office to deliver a cup of coffee or to perform some other personal task, I became angrier and disliked her even more. Because I've never been able to hide my feelings well, over time she sensed that I disliked her and that I resented doing things for her. Consequently, one day she became fed up with my bad attitude and fired me.

That experience and others taught me valuable lessons about the workforce. One of the lessons we parents should

A Brighter Day:
How Parents Can Help African American Youth

share with our children is, "Given the many problems that Black folks face in the United States, we can't afford to behave inappropriately or act unprofessionally in the workplace." Workplace etiquette—how to behave appropriately at work—[1] is very important, and it can determine if an individual will be able to support herself financially or join the ranks of the unemployed. Therefore, in the remainder of this chapter, I share additional ways that we can prepare our youth for the workforce, starting with information about job interviews.

How We Can Prepare Our Youth for Job Interviews

Although an employer may have already formed an opinion of a job candidate from his resume (a document describing the individual's education history, previous work experiences, awards and honors received, references, etc.), the job interview can really determine whether or not he gets the job. A basic strategy that we can use is to teach our youth how to dress and how to prepare for job interviews. Of course, the job applicant should arrive on time. Regardless of the job the individual is seeking, all males should wear a business suit and tie (or at least a dress shirt, dress pants, and tie), and all females should be dressed in a professional manner. But before the applicant even dresses for the interview and shows up, experts say there are several pre-interview steps to take.

According to the Emily Post Institute, the applicant should visit the prospective job site before the actual interview. This will permit the applicant to:

- find out how much time it takes to get to the job site from home
- see how employees in the organization dress
- meet the receptionist ahead of time, learn her name, and ask questions

- pick up informational materials about the company, and
- find out the name of the person who will be interviewing you.[2]

Regarding how to dress for the interview, experts at the Emily Post Institute say:

> In the old days, a coat and tie or suit would usually do the trick. Now, offices run the gamut from shorts and sandals to traditional suits. Do your homework. Either call or visit to find out what the office dress code is. A visit will let you see what your future colleagues wear to work. A good bet is to dress slightly more formally than the average person. In other words, if most people wear slacks and a sport shirt, wear slacks with a coat and tie. Everyone in coat and tie? Wear a suit. Everyone in a suit? Wear your best suit.[3] These experts also offer the following suggestions:
> - Make sure that your shoes are polished and clean.
> - Your clothes should be clean and ironed.
> - Your fingernails should be well groomed.
> - Make sure that your hair is neat.
> - Do not wear too much jewelry.
> - Have copies of your resume ready to hand out.
> - Make sure that you have the correct information about where the interview will take place.
> - Be on time.

A Brighter Day:
How Parents Can Help African American Youth

- Know the name of each person with whom you'll be meeting, and how to pronounce the names correctly.
- Have a pen and paper in order to take notes.
- Dress appropriately for the weather.
- Females should take an extra pair of nylons.[4]

As I read over the above checklist, I thought about how valuable this advice would've been during my high school and college years when I was searching for jobs. One incident that comes to mind occurred during the summer following my junior year of college.

I'd been invited to interview for a summer internship with a major news magazine. Instead of doing the pre-interview work that the Emily Post Institute experts recommend, I relied on my own assumptions. Although I'd never been to the actual job site, I guessed the amount of time it would take to travel by bus from my university apartment. Unfortunately, I ended up having to take several buses to get there, and I arrived more than an hour late.

When I arrived, I apologized to the interviewer, a stern-looking, middle-aged African American man, and explained what had happened. Nevertheless, throughout the interview, it was clear to me that he'd already formed a very negative impression of me. When I left, I felt that I'd blown a great opportunity to help my career and earn a good summer income. I kept hoping and praying that he would have mercy on me and offer me the job anyway, but he didn't.

When he notified me that I hadn't gotten the job, I was heartbroken. I ended up having to take a less prestigious and much lower-paying job for the summer, but I learned an important lesson the hard way: It's important to be on time, if not early, for job interviews. Because "CP Time" (Colored People's Time) is a tradition in Black culture, being on time for interviews and for work is an extremely important concept for our youth to learn while they're young. CP Time says that "It's okay to arrive 20, 30, or 40 minutes late because everyone knows that Black folks are never on time." But in order to get and keep jobs—especially during this current economic crisis—we must realize how important it is for us to be on time, start working on time, and not leave one minute before our work shift ends, *and* we must instill these messages in our youth.

After the job applicant has dressed appropriately and arrived at the interview on time, there are several other actions that must be taken in order to make a good impression—one that will result in a job offer. Sometimes, it's the little things that can ruin a job opportunity. I learned this many years ago when I attended a speech given by an official who was instrumental in hiring faculty and administrators at a community college.

This elderly White woman had a reputation for being a tough, no-nonsense boss. In fact, although she was petite, a lot of people feared her because she loved to brag about her hobby of shooting rifles during her spare time. But something that she said during her talk bothered me. She stated, "I can always tell everything that I need to know about a person by looking him in the eye. If he can't look me in the eye, then I won't hire him!" This statement bothered me because in some cultures and in certain families, children are taught that looking an adult in the eyes is a sign of disrespect. In my own family, for example, when I was growing up, whenever my mother said, "Look me in the eye," she was trying to determine if someone was lying or telling the truth in order to decide who deserved a beating and who didn't. So, from childhood onward, I've had trouble looking people directly in the eye, not because I'm lying, but because it brings back bad memories.

The ability to make direct eye contact is an important part of the job interview process. In fact, it's the first item on the Emily Post Institute's list of recommendations for job interview success. According to the Institute experts, applicants who "do the next five things with everyone [they] meet . . . are well on [their] way to success"[5]:

- "Look them in the eye.
- Give a firm handshake.
- Greet them—'How do you do?' or 'How do you do, Mrs.' _____.
- When saying your name, say it slowly and clearly, and smile!"[6]

How to Succeed on the Job

Once an individual gets a job, if she loves it, if it pays well, and if she has supportive colleagues and a fair and supportive boss, that person should hold on to that job for dear life! In reality, most jobs are imperfect for one reason or another. The key, in my opinion, is to find a way to make the most out of the job situation. This is something I had to tell one of my daughters repeatedly when she had to deal with a racist boss during her years as a college undergraduate. I also had to teach myself this lesson on several occasions when I had jobs I couldn't stand.

The following lessons that I learned from my experiences and shared with my own children may be helpful to you as you prepare African American youth for the workforce:

- No job is perfect.
- Balance working hard and taking care of your health.
- Sometimes, an employee will have to put up with unpleasant situations before she can move to a better job.
- The best ways to deal with toxic bosses are to avoid them whenever possible, watch your back, keep your guard up, and keep a paper trail by documenting inappropriate, racist, and unfair behaviors. The documentation should describe the event that occurred, who was involved, names, dates, and places.
- Sometimes, an employee will have to deal with jealous, racist, petty, and undermining colleagues. The employee should avoid these people as much as possible, try not to socialize with them, gossip with them, eat lunch with them, or allow them to "push her buttons" by provoking her to anger.
- Behave in a professional and respectful manner with all co-workers, even those who are difficult.

We should also inform our youth that they won't be able to get away with what other folks can get away with. Some employees and supervisors engage in unprofessional conduct, arrive late, add more time to their timesheets than what they actually worked, over bill the company, etc. However, African Americans who indulge in any of these practices will probably be penalized or fired, even as others are getting away with these behaviors.

Youth need to also know that if an employee is subjected to racism, sexism, or any other form of discrimination, that individual has the right to contact the Office of Fair Housing and Employment and the Equal Employment Opportunity Commission (EEOC). The EEOC is supposed to enforce numerous laws that protect the civil rights of employees.

A Brighter Day:
How Parents Can Help African American Youth

A Final Word

The final workplace issue that we should address with our youth concerns the use and abuse of power. Throughout my life, I've met lots of rude people. I've been followed and racially profiled in stores by Asian employees and store owners. I've been ignored and treated disrespectfully by White sales clerks, a White airport shuttle driver, White airport employees in New Orleans, White educators in Texas, Minnesota, and California, disrespected by some White graduate students, cursed out by an Asian woman, and made fun of in Spanish by Latinos who didn't know that I knew that they were talking about me. In fact, I can't even begin to remember all of the faces and races of the rude folks I've met. But I do know that rude people come in all races, shapes, sizes, and ages, and some of the rudest people that I've ever met have been Black people who were supposed to be doing their jobs and behaving in a professional manner.

In a Midwestern airport, for example, I watched a gray-haired African American employee chomp on a wad of gum as if she hadn't eaten in days and yell at a White co-worker while customers waited in line. But this woman's behavior was mild in comparison to the rude behaviors I've witnessed or personally experienced from Black airport employees in other regions. In fact, some of the rudest so-called "professional" people that I've ever met are Black employees at an airport in the southwest that I dread going to.

Each of these cases involves the use and abuse of power. Unfortunately, some people simply can't handle power well. Therefore, it is important for us to teach our youth not to let their jobs, titles, or positions go to their heads, and to always treat people respectfully.

Chapter 7

How We Can Help Our Youth Avoid Prison Incarceration

In 1983, I was sitting in my mother's living room, holding my baby daughter and chatting with my grandmother who was visiting from Texas, when a loud commotion startled us. Someone was banging on the front door. When I opened it, a neighbor shouted, "The police are down at the park beating Calvin!" Within minutes, I'd handed my baby to my grandmother, and ran to the park that intersected the San Diego street on which my mother lived. When I got to the park, a small crowd of spectators had gathered around a parked police car.

As I moved closer, I saw an overweight cop sitting on my brother, who was lying face down in the back seat of the car, as another cop struck him repeatedly with his fists. Even though I was out of breath, I began yelling frantically, "Stop beating my brother! Stop hitting him!" But the officers ignored me. Although it was broad daylight and plenty of witnesses were watching, they didn't care. In spite of my screams, they boldly continued to beat my brother. At one point, I began to yell, "I'm calling the news media! I'm calling the NAACP!" All of a sudden, the officers decided it was time to stop. However, instead of releasing my brother, they were apparently planning to drive off with him. I feared that they would take him somewhere and kill him. So before they drove off I screamed, "I can see how many bruises he has on his face. If he ends up with more bruises, we're gonna sue you!"

When they drove away, I ran back to my mother's house and began to make telephone calls. I called the police station

A Brighter Day:
How Parents Can Help African American Youth

and explained what I'd seen, and that I feared the police were planning to kill my brother. Next, I called relatives and the local chapter of the NAACP. Several hours later, my brother was released and returned home to tell his story. I don't remember what he told us about what transpired between the time that he was driven from the park and the time that he came home, but I do remember his account of how the ordeal began. When I heard it, I was amazed by his stupidity.

Calvin, who was 20 years old at the time, said he was minding his business in the park when a police officer approached him and ordered, "Get out of the park!" Instead of leaving, Calvin decided to stand his ground. He told the officer that he had a right to be in the park, he lived down the street, and he wasn't doing anything wrong. Then, when the police officer insulted him and insisted that he leave, Calvin said, "Why don't you take off your gun so we can have a fair fight." At that point, the officer called for backup, and he and his partner decided that they would teach Calvin a lesson by beating him up.

When Calvin told me this story, I lost a lot of sympathy for him. The police were definitely wrong for trying to make him leave a public park in his own neighborhood and for assaulting him, but he had acted stupidly when he challenged an armed member of law enforcement to a fight, especially when the San Diego Police Department already had a reputation for routinely driving into predominantly Black neighborhoods and harassing African American males. In the past, I had personally seen the police driving down our street, picking on some of the Black boys in the neighborhood and shouting at residents to stop watching from their own living room windows. In fact, I'd even written an essay about how the police behaved in our community. This essay was published in a local newspaper.

Chapter 7: How We Can Help Our Youth Avoid Prison Incarceration

The police who patrolled our neighborhood were bold, brazen, and notoriously racist. These were three good reasons why Calvin should have merely left the park when the cop told him to do so. But there were several other reasons why my brother shouldn't have challenged that cop to a fight. First, Calvin was a well-known gang member. Second, he was already addicted to crack cocaine at the time. Third, he already had an arrest and incarceration record. All of these reasons could easily have been used as ammunition to send him back to jail or to give the police an excuse to murder him.

Decades have passed since the day when I saw the police beating my brother, and I still get sad when I think about it. Calvin has been dead for 11 years, and the man who eventually murdered him is probably already free and walking the streets. Since the day when Calvin was beaten, countless other African American teens and adults have experienced police brutality. In some cases, the beatings and deaths could've been avoided. In others, nothing could've been done. Because most African American youth will have to deal with the police and other law enforcers at some point in their lives, it is important for us as parents to teach them some basic lessons that I've learned. Throughout the remainder of this chapter, I share several lessons, research, and related stories. I'll start with what we must teach our youth about law enforcement, and then speak about incarceration.

What We Should Teach Our Youth About Police and Other Law Enforcement Agents

Because African Americans have had a difficult history with law enforcement, many Black children are reared to believe that anyone who wears a police officer's or sheriff's deputy uniform is a bad guy. One of my husband's closest friends, an African American law enforcement officer, once

A Brighter Day:
How Parents Can Help African American Youth

told me this. One day, while he was driving through a predominantly Black Los Angeles neighborhood, he waved at a little Black boy. In an instant, the child's mother grabbed the boy and snarled at the officer, "He ain't got nothing to say to you!" The woman didn't even want her son to wave back because she obviously viewed the officer negatively. The officer who told me this story was troubled by this parent's behavior and believed that she was setting a bad example for her son. I agreed with him. What harm would it have done if the boy had merely waved back after the officer said "hello?" None whatsoever.

Although the Black community has suffered a long history of police brutality, racism, and other forms of police corruption, it's still important for us to teach our children the true purpose of law enforcement and to deal wisely with officers. Here are several things that youth should know:

- Law enforcement agents are hired to protect and serve the community. That includes Black folks!
- There are some good police officers and sheriff's deputies and some bad ones. Because the Black community has had such a long negative history with law enforcement, it is important that parents use wisdom when teaching children how to view officers. When we teach our youth that "They're all corrupt, racist, and bad," we are wrong because not all are this way. There are exceptions to every rule.
- Treat all law enforcement agents respectfully.
- Do not argue with law enforcement. In *Law for Dummies: A Reference for the Rest of Us!* John Ventura says that suspects who argue with the police increase their chances of being brutalized.[1]

Chapter 7: How We Can Help Our Youth Avoid Prison Incarceration

- If youth are questioned by law enforcement, they should only say what is absolutely necessary because anything that they say will probably be used against them.

- If youth run from the police or try to resist arrest, they will increase their chances of getting beaten.[2] The late, celebrated, African American attorney, Johnny Cochran, said that many of the African American men that he saw in court had been beaten by police for "failing the attitude test." In other words, they were beaten because they were deemed to have a bad attitude.[3]

There is no excuse for a law enforcement agent to beat a suspect—unless it's for the purpose of self-defense—and there is no guarantee that racist, sadistic, weak, and insecure officers won't beat even the most well behaved suspects. However, the point that I'm trying to make is that having a bad attitude, resisting arrest, and being rude will only increase the likelihood that suspects—especially African Americans—will be beaten. This is an important message for us to teach our youth.

What Youth Need to Know About Driving While Black

According to the U. S. Department of Justice, in 2005, nearly 44 million people "had face-to-face contact with police," and the most common reason involved a traffic stop, usually for speeding.[4] The U. S. Department of Justice, a division of the United States government also admitted that during traffic stops, police are more likely to search Black and Hispanic drivers than White drivers, police are twice as likely to arrest Black drivers, especially Black males, than Whites, and police are more likely to use force against Blacks and Hispanics. In other words, this government agency has

A Brighter Day:
How Parents Can Help African American Youth

admitted that racism is rampant in law enforcement and it is not a figment of the Black community's imagination. Although African American parents and children are no match for the deeply entrenched racist practices that are common in this country, especially among law enforcement agents, there are several things that we parents can do that may possibly decrease the likelihood that our children will be brutalized or even killed by corrupt and racist law enforcement agents.

Here are several tips that we should share with our youth *before* they begin to drive:

- Do not give law enforcement an excuse to mistreat you. For example, since speeding is the main reason why police stop drivers, if you speed, you are not only giving law enforcement a legitimate reason to pull you over, but you may be setting in motion a negative chain of events that could result in hospitalization or death.
- Driving under the influence of alcohol or drugs is definitely out of the question.
- Do not drive with a suspended license.
- Do your best to always obey all traffic rules.
- Failing to obey even apparently "minor" traffic laws can be detrimental.
- Keep your vehicle in good condition. According to the U. S. Department of Justice, some type of "vehicle defect" is the third most common reason why police stop drivers.[5]

What to Teach Youth About the Consequences of Drug Use and Selling Drugs

The introduction of crack cocaine into the Black community in recent decades was simply disastrous to African American families. The cheap price of crack made it easier for low-income people to purchase cocaine, and by the 1980s, Black families across the nation were suffering its ill effects. Today, many African American children in foster care are there because of parents who got hooked on crack or some other drug, and many African American youth and adults are caught up in the prison pipeline for the same reason.

The easy availability of drugs in low-income Black communities has led to the stereotype that most African Americans buy or sell drugs.[6] The truth is that "five times as many Whites use drugs" as minorities.[7] Although Whites are more likely to use drugs than African Americans, the stereotype about Blacks and drug use and drug selling persists, and this is one of the main reasons why police and other law enforcement agents engage in racial profiling.

Obviously, getting involved with buying, selling, or using illegal drugs is one of the deadliest mistakes our youth can make. Youth who use drugs run the risk of earning poor grades, developing mental and physical problems, having poor relationships with their peers, having violent outbursts, and getting arrested.[8]

Although drug use among youth declined somewhat in recent years, in 2005, more than two million youth needed treatment for drug or alcohol abuse, and some were as young as 12 years old.[9] This means that parents shouldn't wait until youth are in middle school or high school to start educating them about the consequences of drug use and drug selling. We must start when they are young.

Sharing the following messages can be helpful to our youth:

- We must practice what we preach. The old "Do as I say, not as I do" model of parenting is hypocritical and counterproductive. One of the best ways to almost guarantee that a child will use drugs or alcohol is for a parent to model these behaviors at home. When a parent engages in these behaviors, children learn what is and isn't acceptable. Moreover, having these substances in the home gives the child easy access to them. How many children have rolled up a sheet of paper and pretended to smoke a cigarette to imitate mom or dad?

- Marijuana is not harmless, and using it can lead to a desire for more hard core drugs.
- Teach youth about the side effects of drugs, especially crack cocaine. This is extremely important because of its prevalence in Black communities. Children as young as 12 years old have been known to use crack[10], and crack use is one of the main reasons why African Americans get trapped in the prison system. Among the side effects of crack are "acute respiratory problems including coughing, shortness of breath, and severe chest pains with lung trauma and bleeding."[11]
- Teach children that they will probably be offered drugs at school, so they should be prepared to say "no" when this happens. According to the U. S. Department of Justice, "In 2005, 25% of all students in grades 9 through 12 reported that someone had offered, sold, or given them an illegal drug on school property."[12]
- Tell youth that if they choose to sell drugs, they will increase their chances of being stopped, profiled, and arrested by law enforcement agents. The FBI reported that in 2005, "there were 141,035 juveniles (under the age of 18) arrested by state and local law enforcement agencies for drug abuse violations. . . ."[13]

Chapter 7: How We Can Help Our Youth Avoid Prison Incarceration

- We must encourage our youth to join and stay involved in *legal* extracurricular activities. Youth who participate in extracurricular activities, such as "band, sports, student government, or dance lessons," are less likely to use illegal drugs.[14]

Advice from a Veteran African American Police Officer

As I was working on this chapter, I had the opportunity to have a down-to-earth telephone conversation with a veteran African American police officer, whom I'll refer to as "Nora." Nora has worked as a police officer in a predominantly Black and Latino city in Los Angeles County for 10 years. Because she, her mother, and I go to the same beauty shop, we've known each other for years and have had many interesting discussions. When I told Nora's mother that I was writing a book for African American parents and wanted her daughter's perspective on what they should know about the police, the mother urged her daughter to telephone me. My conversation with Nora gave me additional information that I want to share with you.

One of the main points that Nora wanted me to tell parents is that we shouldn't be naïve about how our children dress, behave, and with whom they associate. She explained:

> A lot of Black parents are naïve about their children's activities. If your straight "A" AP [Advanced Placement] student is dressing like a gang member, the officer who sees him walking down the street looks at him like he's a gang member, not a straight "A" student. Parents need to be more aware of pop culture. Their children may be a model student, but if they don't have the appearance of that, then that might get the attention of a police officer.

A Brighter Day:
How Parents Can Help African American Youth

Nora also said that racism is indeed common in law enforcement, but not all acts that African Americans view as racist are racially motivated. Some are based on the cultural ignorance of police officers, and others are based on cases of mistaken identity. To emphasize her point about mistaken identity, Nora told me a story about an incident that occurred when she and her partner, another African American female, were on patrol. The officers received a radio call that an armed robbery had just been committed by a Black male fitting a certain description and driving a certain car. A few minutes later, the officers saw a Black male who fit the description, and they pulled him over. According to Nora:

> The very first thing out of his mouth was that we stopped him because he was Black. First, we patted him down. After determining that he didn't have a weapon, we explained to him why we stopped him, but he didn't believe it. Then I sat him in the police car, had him read the terminal, and he said, "That sounds just like me!" Then, he apologized to us.
>
> I've been in physical altercations, but it wasn't because the person was Black; it was a good guy-bad guy issue, not a Black-White or Black-Brown issue.

Nora was candid about the existence of racism in law enforcement. "Racism does exist," she said. "I think that schools and higher education are inherently racist. White people do not associate us with [Whites]. It's deeply ingrained in their subconscious." Nora also acknowledged that many White cops are terrified of African Americans, especially Black males. "Rodney King got beat because they [the police officers] were scared to death," she said. At the same time, however, Nora insisted that many acts that appear to be racially

Chapter 7: How We Can Help Our Youth Avoid Prison Incarceration

motivated stem from cultural ignorance and a lack of proper training of law enforcement agents. "In the police academy, you receive cultural awareness training for every group—except for Black culture," she said. So, a lot of the negative interactions between police and African Americans are "[based on] ignorance, not racism." To illustrate her point, she described the following case that involved a Hispanic officer that she was training:

> We got a call about a loud disturbance. When we arrived, I saw a group of Black males playing dominoes. I know as a culture we can get loud, but the Hispanic officer wanted to call for back up. What I saw was just four guys playing dominoes. What he saw was a threat. I said, "Hey guys, keep it down." They said "thanks," and that was it.

Afterwards, Nora questioned the Hispanic officer about his reaction. He admitted that he had been fearful and had never been around Blacks. His gut reaction—to immediately call for assistance—was rooted in the stereotypes that he held about Blacks. Also, in the police academy, he hadn't received any training about Black culture.

Nora also wanted African American parents to know how our children should behave if they are detained by police. She said that we should tell our youth the following:

> If you are stopped, be respectful. Be polite, and afterwards ask the officer why he stopped you. There is a fine line. You are polite, but you also have First Amendment rights. You can ask to speak with an officer's sergeant, and you can go to the police department and file a complaint. If you are armed with information, you'll be safer and more secure.

A Brighter Day:
How Parents Can Help African American Youth

In the remainder of this chapter I share ways that we can decrease our children's chances of getting incarcerated. The fact remains that African Americans continue to be wrongfully convicted more often than Whites and given stiffer sentences than those accused of the same offenses or even more serious crimes. We must never forget these lessons while teaching our children about the American judicial system.

We Must Teach Our Children that the Road to Prison Can Start Very Early.

One of the most important lessons that we must instill in our children is that "The road to prison can start very early"— and we parents must make sure that we aren't leading our children down that road through our own actions.

Instead of receiving counseling and being taught alternatives to inappropriate behavior, many children are being incarcerated at a very young age. "Sentencing Children to Die in Prison," a shocking report that the Equal Justice Initiative released in late 2007, revealed that not only are children being incarcerated at an early age, but numerous 13- and 14-year-old youth have been tried as adults and sentenced to life in prison.[15] One of the most appalling details of the report is that some of the youth who received life sentences "were charged with crimes that do not involve homicide or even injury."[16] Given the judicial system's racist history, it shouldn't surprise us that Black children are more likely than Whites, Latinos, and others to be sentenced to life in prison. A clear message in this report is that problems at home, such as poor parenting, often result in youth ending up in prison later in life. Throughout this book, I've repeatedly emphasized that child abuse can lead to many long-term problems for youth. This message also surfaced in another startling report, "America's Cradle to Prison Pipeline," which was issued by the Children's Defense Fund. According to this powerful report:

- Abused and neglected children are far more likely to be delinquent and arrested as adults.
- Children in the juvenile justice system are more likely to have a history of child abuse and neglect than children outside the system.
- Poor children are more likely to be abused or neglected. They are also more likely to be placed in foster care.[17]
- Children of color are more likely to be incarcerated in both the juvenile and criminal justice systems.[18]
- One in three Black boys born in 2001 will spend time in prison at some point in their lives.[19]
- Boys adjudicated delinquent for a violent offense between ages 10 and 16 were more than 6 times as likely to be convicted of a violent crime by age 24.[20]

This research clearly shows that there is a strong link between child abuse and future criminality. A story that I know quite well illustrates this point. It involved an African American boy who attended the same church that I attended when I was growing up.

This boy's mother and my mother were good friends, and eventually we all ended up attending the same church. At church, the woman's son was usually quiet and kept to himself. Later, he ended up dating one of my family members. After his mother died of cancer at a relatively young age, our family lost touch with him. Many years later, I was shocked to hear of his fate. He'd been arrested, tried, and convicted of raping

A Brighter Day:
How Parents Can Help African American Youth

and murdering an elderly White woman. Instead of being sentenced to death, he received a life sentence. This story troubled me for a long time. What had happened to the quiet boy that I used to see at church? How could he have committed such horrible crimes when he apparently was raised by a loving mother who provided all of his needs and tried to instill good values in him?

One day when I was discussing this case with my mother during a telephone conversation, she gave me the answer I'd been searching for. When the boy was very young, his mother had married a man who appeared to be the perfect stepfather. This man was so attached to her son that he didn't want the boy to sleep alone. So, the stepfather often slept with the child. It took some time—too long, unfortunately—for the naïve mother to realize that she'd married a child molester. The damage that was done to her son during childhood surfaced after her death when he was arrested for a crime that sealed his fate. As far as I know, he will eventually die in prison.

I shared this story to emphasize another message that I've repeated throughout this book: Parents must be highly selective about the people that they allow around their children. Single mothers who are desperate for male companionship aren't wise when they let boyfriends move into the house or marry men who are really after their kids. The road to prison for many African American youth begins when parents bring predators into the home. Later, many of these children retaliate by abusing others or lashing out at society in other ways. Sometimes, their cries for help or this lashing out in anger surfaces in school, a point that I will say more about in the next section.

Chapter 7: How We Can Help Our Youth Avoid Prison Incarceration

A Child's Behavior at School is Often a Warning Sign that She is Headed Down the Path to Prison.

In my line of work (I teach at a university and give presentations and workshops for educators and parents), I often hear complaints about the way African American children behave in school. I mentioned earlier that many educators believe that Black children don't know how to behave properly at school. As a result, they are more likely to be suspended and expelled from school than other children. In fact, on average, more than one million Black children are suspended from school each year, and more than 30,000 are expelled. I won't repeat all of the reasons why this happens, but what I want to emphasize in this chapter is that it's important for parents and youth to know that the path to prison often begins in school. Many adults who ended up in prison exhibited warning signs—bad behavior in school—when they were children.

Recent research has documented that there is actually a "school-to-prison pipeline."[21] Researchers for the NAACP Legal Defense and Educational Fund refer to the pipeline as "a one-way path toward prison" as a result of policies that "push children out of school and hasten their entry into the juvenile, and eventually the criminal, justice system, where prison is the end of the road."[22]

Parents should be aware that suspension can have short- and long-term consequences for our children. Therefore, we need to do everything possible to prevent them from being suspended and expelled from school. Starting early is crucial, for "Even pre-schoolers, who can hardly be said to pose a danger to classmates or staff, have been suspended or expelled in increasing numbers."[23] In other words, it is extremely

A Brighter Day:
How Parents Can Help African American Youth

important for us to have high expectations and strict guidelines about how our children should behave in school, and we must instill this information in our youth before they start preschool. Then, we must continue to share this message with them throughout their K–12 schooling.

Sharing the following practical advice with our children may help them stay out of trouble:

- Follow all school rules.
- If gum chewing isn't allowed, don't take gum to school, and don't ask other students for gum.
- If another student is breaking a school rule, don't be a follower. Continue to do the right thing because although the other student may not get caught, you probably will.
- Don't talk in class without permission.
- Don't get out of your seat in class or the cafeteria without permission.
- Don't talk back to the teacher, no matter how wrong you think he/she is.
- If you believe that a teacher or school administrator is treating you unfairly, don't try to handle the situation alone. Tell your parent.
- If anyone bullies you, tell your parent.
- Don't start fights or arguments or pick on other students.
- Mind your own business as much as possible.
- Keep your hands to yourself.
- Watch what you say to other students and adults, because what you say may be misunderstood, used against you, or viewed as threatening or even as sexual harassment.

Chapter 7: How We Can Help Our Youth Avoid Prison Incarceration

- Do not use profanity, sexually explicit language, or offensive terms to refer to males or females. (Parents should be specific about telling youth which words can get them into trouble, even if other students use them and even if these words are popular in rap and other types of music. Also, parents will, hopefully, practice what we preach and not use these words ourselves. If we're cursing at our children, then we shouldn't be surprised when they curse at other children.)
- If you finish your class work early, stay in your seat, keep your mouth shut, read a book or magazine, or ask permission to work on other class assignments.
- If you get called into the school office or are suspended from school, be as cooperative as possible. Otherwise, you might get arrested and have even more serious accusations made against you.

As I mentioned previously, we should also make sure that our children have strong reading and math skills. Struggling students often misbehave in school to hide the fact that they can't read well or that they lack basic math skills. Having poor reading skills is linked to many problems in school and during adulthood. If your child is struggling with reading or math, ask the teacher and school administrators for help. Also, look for community-based tutoring programs to assist your child. Many churches have developed free tutoring programs.

We must also teach our children alternatives to fighting at school. Fighting is one of the main reasons why so many African American children get suspended and expelled from school. The way each parent chooses to handle this problem is personal. In my own case, I told my three children to never start a fight, to avoid fighting at all costs, but in the case of

A Brighter Day:
How Parents Can Help African American Youth

self-defense, to protect and defend themselves. Unfortunately, in the era of "Zero Tolerance" policies, the child who hits back in self-defense will also be suspended from school. I don't agree with this aspect of Zero Tolerance because it is hypocritical and unrealistic. Nevertheless, since it is widely enforced in schools throughout the nation, we must do our best to help our children think of alternatives to fighting.

We Must Teach Our Children that Jail, Juvenile Hall, and Prison are not Nice Places.

Parents should also tell youth that in jail, juvenile hall, and prison, everything is controlled by authorities, including what and how much to eat, when to wake up and go to bed, when to take a shower, when to exercise, and when and how often an inmate can talk on the telephone and have visitors. In many ways, being an inmate is like being a slave with very few rights and very little freedom. If the inmate happens to get sick while incarcerated, that individual will still be treated like an inmate—an individual with few rights. The following story about a 42-year-old African American inmate is a good example of this point.

In May 2004, a man lay in bed, smiling at his three visitors. He was relieved to see them because he'd been afraid that they wouldn't come. "I didn't think anybody loved me," he said. "I'm surprised you guys came." In spite of his smile, the tan walls couldn't hide the fact that the room was very old and quite dirty. Even the sunlight beaming through the tiny window couldn't brighten up this drab room in a prison infirmary. A tray of untouched food sat near his bedside. Each time that he spoke, a huge tumor bulged from the left side of his neck. Earlier that day, a prison nurse had notified the visitors—the inmate's mother, sister, and brother-in-law—that he was dying, and he wanted to see them. At the time, the inmate knew that his cancer had returned, but he didn't know that he was actually dying.

For awhile, the small group talked about unimportant things. Then, the patient complained that he was cold and thirsty and rang for the nurse. A middle-aged Black woman finally arrived, and when she did, she didn't bother to hide her irritation. "What do you want, Harris?" she demanded. "Can I have a blanket and some water?" he replied sweetly. "Look, Harris, don't start acting crazy just because you have visitors," the nurse scolded. "You know that even though this is an infirmary, it's a prison first!" Before leaving the room, she turned to the inmate's mother and asked, "Sometimes, don't you wish that you had flushed your kids down the toilet?" The nurse clearly meant it as a joke, but the visitors were appalled by her lack of professionalism. The inmate's mother was too shocked to even reply to this woman's tactless joke. After all, what could she say? If she told the nurse that she was offended by her comment, who knows what she would've done to the inmate after the visitors left? The nurse had already made it clear that she was the boss. If the inmate rubbed her the wrong way, she could take her time administering pain medication and giving him food, water, and a blanket. And take her time she did, for it took quite awhile for her to bring the blanket and water that he requested.

Unlike many of the stories that I've described in this book, this one didn't come second hand. Not only did I witness the above scene with my own eyes, but that day marked the beginning of a long ordeal that directly involved me. Although I was shocked and disgusted by the nurse's behavior, the facts were obvious: My younger brother Jeffery was dying, he was in prison, and in prison, some inmates—even dying ones—

A Brighter Day:
How Parents Can Help African American Youth

are treated worse than dogs. This was the lesson that I learned that day. During the next six weeks, I would be reminded of this lesson time and time again. I also quickly learned that despite the fact that Jeffery had been arrested for a drug-related, nonviolent offense, no one in the prison system cared that my brother was dying, and prison employees had little, if any, respect or sympathy for family members who tried to visit him. In fact, whenever I tried to visit him in the hospital prison ward where he was eventually transferred—as a guard stood watch over the room 24 hours a day— or the dingy prison infirmary, I was reminded of the fact that inmates are similar to slaves.

Each visit took a heavy emotional and psychological toll on me as guards treated me like I was less than human. Even though I have multiple degrees and have never been arrested, in their eyes my crimes were (1) I had a brother who was an inmate, and (2) I had the audacity to insist that I and other family members be permitted to visit him during his final weeks on this earth. In fact, during one of my visits, an African American guard told me that we were spoiling my brother by trying to visit him in the hospital. Other guards said that Jeffery was faking, and even though he had stage-four cancer, in their opinion, he wasn't sick enough to deserve regular visits from family members. Whenever I called to inquire about Jeffery's condition, a White prison nurse constantly reminded me that "inmates are the scum of the earth" who deserve to suffer.

Throughout those weeks, I wrote letters of complaint to prison officials and made numerous calls about how prison employees treated Jeffery, other family members, and me, but the guards and prison nurses found creative ways to constantly remind us that they were in charge, and like slaves, inmates have few rights. Interestingly, because Jeffery had already been

168

incarcerated numerous times for shoplifting and selling drugs, he seemed less disturbed than the rest of us by the inhumane way in which he was treated.

About three weeks after my mother and I learned that Jeffery was dying, a family member decided to play hard ball with him; she told Jeffery that his cancer was terminal and that he needed to "get right with God." That's when everything changed. My brother's upbeat attitude, joking, and optimism turned into depression and resignation. He stopped eating. Whenever I visited him, his breakfast and lunch trays would be covered in plastic, as if he hadn't eaten a single bite. I begged him to eat. Once in awhile he would glare at me and drink a protein drink just to shut me up. Sometimes he would look at me defiantly out of his one good eye—the other was clouded over by an untreated cataract—and just stare at me as if he couldn't hear me or couldn't stand me.

One day when I was visiting, Jeffery told the guard that he needed to use the restroom. When the guard walked over to his bed and pulled the cover off of him, two things shocked me: My brother's formally tall and muscular body had withered away to skin and bones. But the most shocking thing of all was that one of his bony legs was shackled to the bed by handcuffs. More than any other incident that had previously occurred, this incident—watching a guard unshackle a leg that could barely walk—reminded me of how similar his fate was to that of a slave.

Six weeks after the prison nurse informed us that my brother was dying, Jeffery died in the middle of the night. By then, he had been transferred from the hospital back to the prison infirmary. Prison officials felt it was too expensive to keep a dying man who refused to eat in a hospital, so they decided to let him starve to death in the prison infirmary

169

A Brighter Day:
How Parents Can Help African American Youth

instead. My family and I weren't surprised when he finally died, but we learned that even in death an inmate has no dignity and can't be viewed or treated humanely. Jeffery's body went missing for several hours. My mother had to battle with the coroner's office not only to locate the body but to get it released and transferred to our hometown for burial.

For my two surviving siblings, my mother, and me, Jeffery's death was more than just the death of a family member. For my mother, his death marked the demise of her firstborn son, a child whose birth she had prayed for. In fact, she had promised God that if He gave her a son—after she'd had three girls in a row—she would dedicate him to God. Her dream of seeing Jeffery become a preacher never materialized. For my two surviving sisters and me, our last brother was gone. As I mentioned previously, my brother Calvin, who was younger than Jeffery, had been murdered six years earlier. My sister Tammie had died three years before Calvin. For my mother, Jeffery's death meant that she no longer had any sons; for my sisters and me, his death meant that we no longer had any brothers.

Although my brothers' deaths were tragic to my family and me, their stories aren't unique. Lots of African Americans have lost sons, daughters, siblings, or other relatives to the prison pipeline. But Calvin Marshall and Jeffery Harris weren't just statistics or sensational media stories to me. Calvin was more than a drug-addicted gang member, and Jeffery was more than a drug-addicted petty thief. They were my younger and only brothers. The same mother reared us in the same household, and they were just as intelligent—if not more so—than me. But our lives turned out very differently. Today, I am an accomplished author, tenured professor at a prestigious university, popular workshop presenter, much-

Chapter 7: How We Can Help Our Youth Avoid Prison Incarceration

sought after education consultant, and the married mother of three college students, but my brothers were considered failures when they died. How did the cute little boys who often got on my nerves when we were growing up and who had so much talent become "monsters" and failures by society's standards? Instead of becoming the great African American men that they could have become, how did they become slaves to the revolving doors of the prison pipeline? During the last few years, I've spent a lot of time trying to answer these questions, and I've realized that there is no single answer. Several factors played a role in how my brothers ended up, and the factors that caused us to follow different paths surfaced during childhood. In the next section, I explain these factors because they contain lessons that African American parents can use to help youth avoid my brothers' fates.

What Parents and Guardians Can Learn from My Brothers' Lives and Deaths
Childhood Differences

If people had made predictions about the fates of my brothers and me during our early childhood, I'm sure that many would've concluded that I, not them, would've turned out badly. I say this because during childhood, I was a thief and a problematic student. When two of my sisters and I were little girls, we often stole candy from local grocery stores. I probably would've continued to steal each time that my mother sent us to the grocery store if a traumatic event hadn't occurred to stop me when I was still in elementary school.

One evening, my mother sent two of my sisters to a local store that was run by a White man and his son. But only one of my sisters returned home. The sister who returned was trembling and in tears as she informed my mother that the

A Brighter Day:
How Parents Can Help African American Youth

store owner wouldn't let our other sister come home until my mother went to the store to speak with him. It turned out that while one sister was getting the groceries, the other had been stealing half of an ice cream sandwich—a plan they'd hatched before they entered the store. What they didn't know was that the store owner had watched them. He saw one of them break the ice cream bar in half and slip the other half into her coat pocket. He quickly grabbed the thief and sent the other one home to fetch our mother whom he knew as a friendly but extremely strict parent.

I don't know what happened when my mother got to the store, but I'll never forget what happened when she returned home. She beat both of my sisters so badly that their yelps and screams seemed to fill the apartment for hours. After witnessing the beatings that left my sisters weak, bruised, and traumatized, I vowed that I would never steal again. I wasn't afraid of the police, nor was I afraid of the store owner or his son. I was terrified that my mother would kill me if she ever caught me stealing, and this fear motivated me to kick the habit of stealing, cold turkey! Unfortunately, my brothers were either too young to realize what had happened to my sisters, or they later forgot the brutal beatings that my sisters received that night. I say this because both of them stole things when they got older, and one even committed an armed robbery that we heard about later.

Church

A second big difference between my life and my brothers' is that when I was in elementary school, my mother started sending the three eldest kids—my two sisters and me—to church on a regular basis. The stories about hellfire and

172

Chapter 7: How We Can Help Our Youth Avoid Prison Incarceration

damnation taught in our little Pentecostal churches frightened me and made me want to go to heaven when I died. When I was in third grade, I dedicated my life to God and even dreamed of becoming a nun (I didn't realize that Catholics could become nuns but Pentecostals couldn't). I literally believed everything I heard from the preachers and wanted to follow the church's teachings no matter how hard they were. When I made mistakes, fought with my siblings, or did anything wrong, I would criticize myself and fear that I was going to hell. But I also learned to develop the habit of praying about problems, and this became a life-long coping tool that I continue to rely on today.

I also loved the fact that being at church gave me a legitimate excuse to get out of the house, allowed me to make new friends, and enabled me to become involved in a lot of fun activities. Joining the choir was one of the highlights of my childhood. Even though I have a terrible singing voice (or so I've been told), singing inspirational songs, traveling to other churches to sing with the choir, and attending choir rehearsals made me very happy. For a short time when he was about 13 years old, my brother Jeffery got saved and also became very involved in our church, but his involvement didn't last long. I feel a lot of guilt about that now. At the time, I felt he was stepping on my turf. Over the years, I'd earned the reputation of being the church girl in the family, and I resented the fact that he wanted to follow me around, especially when the choir traveled to other churches and out of town. Instead of encouraging him to attend church functions, I sometimes went out of my way to keep him from going. Jeffery eventually lost interest in church and stopped going completely.

A Brighter Day:
How Parents Can Help African American Youth

In addition to becoming a safe haven for me and an excuse to get away from home often, the church also provided me with several outstanding role models. I watched the behavior of couples who appeared to be happily married, and I studied mothers and fathers who treated their children humanely. When I was in elementary school, Johnny and Patricia, a childless young couple, grew fond of me and wanted to become my godparents. However, fearing that they might have ulterior motives, my mother wouldn't agree to this no matter how much I cried and begged her to let them become my godparents. Even though I eventually lost contact with them after I joined another church that was closer to our home, I never forgot their kindness and the fact that they chose me and made me feel special at a time when I felt ugly and worthless.

Two other church members who made a strong positive impact on me were Brother Bill and Brother Whitson, young ministers at one of the churches that I attended. These men were always kind and encouraging. They told me that I was smart and had potential, and they were proud of my school accomplishments. Years later, during my freshman year of college, Brother Whitson and his wife drove over 100 miles to visit me. The kindness that these ministers and other church members showed me, made it easier for me to endure a painful childhood.

Home Factors

Although the same mother reared my brothers and me in the same household, our experiences at home were very different for a number of reasons. My mother had six children. The three older children, of whom I am one, were reared differently than the three younger children, which included my brothers. As the second eldest child in the family, at an early age, I became responsible for many chores. As I mentioned earlier, while still in elementary school, I was required to comb my hair and my two younger sisters' hair before we went to school. I ironed clothes, washed dishes, did the laundry, babysat, cooked various dishes, helped my brother Jeffery with his homework, and did other chores when I was still quite young. I also think that my mother was much stricter on the three older children than the three younger ones.

In addition to the age differences between my brothers and me, gender also mattered. Boys were viewed as dirty and unclean, and we learned this lesson early in life. The boys could take out the trash and do "dirty work," but they couldn't wash dishes. Unfortunately, this message affected all of the kids in our family. There was a lot of infighting, bullying, and sibling rivalry among us. When my brothers got old enough to stand up for themselves and grew taller than their three older, bossy sisters, they started to defend themselves. Jeffery and my sister Tammie never got along with each other because apparently Tammie never recovered from the fact that Jeffery was the baby "who pushed her out of the way." In other words, she was the baby of the family until Jeffery was born, and I don't think she ever got over the sibling rivalry that started with his birth. As they grew older, they often had fierce arguments. When they became teenagers, I would always side with Tammie because I had subconsciously adopted the belief that "boys were bad." Of course, today, I am very ashamed to admit this and feel great remorse about the role that I played in mistreating our brothers during their childhood. No matter how many good things I did for them or how many times I

A Brighter Day:
How Parents Can Help African American Youth

was supportive and kind to them—including during their numerous incarcerations—nothing can erase my sorrow, regret, and shame over the mean things that I did to them out of ignorance, selfishness, and misplaced loyalty.

Another home factor that had a great and negative impact on my brothers was the fact that both grew up without a positive male role model at home. The man who later became our stepfather was very intelligent. He could speak French and had planned to become an attorney. He was also very kind, encouraging, and fun loving. But his dreams were destroyed by alcoholism, and he rarely stood up for himself in a home where verbal and physical abuse were common. Therefore, in spite of his good qualities, he failed to become the strong male role model that his young, impressionable, and emotionally vulnerable stepsons needed.

Moreover, Jeffery's father (who was also my father) lived hundreds of miles away and rarely telephoned or came to visit before he eventually drowned when I was 13 years old. Calvin's father, who lived in the same city in which we lived, rarely took an interest in his son's well-being. For a while, during elementary school, Jeffery lived in San Francisco with our father. Once when Jeffery lay dying in the prison infirmary, I asked him what he remembered about that period. He said "Daddy" used to take him to watch sports events but also beat him frequently for wetting the bed and for doing poorly in school. In fact, while he was living with my father, Jeffery flunked first grade. When he moved back in with us, he would hide food in his bed as if he'd been deprived. He had also developed a stammer. Today, I believe that not having a positive male role model at home affected my brothers more negatively than it did me.

Chapter 7: How We Can Help Our Youth Avoid Prison Incarceration

Another home factor that contributed to my brothers' demise was that they had less supervision than I had. Less supervision meant more freedom, and more freedom meant that the vices that they were experimenting with weren't detected until it was too late. In Calvin's case, it was easy for him to join a gang and experiment with drugs without being detected. In Jeffery's case, it was easier for him to sell marijuana during his teenage years and get away with it.

School Factors

Our school experiences also played a role in how I ended up and how my brothers ended up. Because of the five-and-a-half-years age difference between Calvin and me, I don't remember much about his experiences at all. In two of the elementary school photos that I still have, he was a dark-chocolate colored boy with curly hair and a beautiful smile. At home, he was a quiet, sensitive, and extremely nervous child who had a quick temper. I always suspected that his nervousness and bad temper came from the fact that while my mother was pregnant with him, she was brutally attacked and disfigured by a knife-carrying assailant who almost murdered her.

Recently, I learned that when he was in elementary school, educators recommended that Calvin take mind-altering medications to calm him down. Whether his chronic anxiety and drug addiction were caused by the medications that were given to my mother to save her life when Calvin was still in her womb or from the psychotropic drugs given to him during childhood, I don't know. Interestingly, research has found that children who are placed on psychotropic drugs during childhood often end up becoming drug addicts during adulthood.

A Brighter Day:
How Parents Can Help African American Youth

Ironically and tragically, while my mother was pregnant with Calvin, she was attacked with a knife, and years later Calvin was stabbed to death. He wasn't shot or beaten to death, but stabbed to death. While he was still in the womb, a knife played an important role in his life, and in his last moments on earth, a knife was involved.

Because Jeffery and I were closer in age—four years apart—I remember more about his K–12 experiences. In fact, we had a lot in common. Like me, Jeffery flunked first grade, and from that point on, he was viewed as being dumb or slow. Both of us talked a lot, and Jeffery was great at telling jokes and making people laugh. Our grades weren't that good, but when I was older, my mother expected me to help him with his homework. I remember trying to help him read, and becoming very frustrated by his lack of progress and his stuttering as he tried to sound out homework assignments.

Jeffery was functionally illiterate when he died. Like many African American K–12 students, he was merely passed through the system with weak skills that weren't corrected during his childhood because of the low expectations of some educators. Although I developed strong reading skills and became an avid reader at an early age, I could have easily been passed through the system in the same way. From kindergarten through fifth grade, most of my teachers viewed me in a negative way. Because of my excessive talking in class, I was labeled a discipline problem and felt that most of my teachers didn't like me. The turning point occurred in sixth grade when I had a teacher who changed my life. She had high expectations of me. She treated me as if I were smart, and she encouraged me to go to college. I could be wrong, but I doubt that either of my brothers ever had such a caring teacher during their childhood.

Chapter 7: How We Can Help Our Youth Avoid Prison Incarceration

The Deadly Combination

When I combine all of the factors that contributed to how my brothers lived and died, I believe that it wasn't merely one factor but a combination. Home factors, such as verbal and physical abuse; not having a strong male role model during childhood; having too much freedom and not being supervised enough during adolescence; not having the strong spiritual foundation or positive role models that I found in churches; their K-12 school experiences; and of course, gravitating to the wrong peers and getting involved with drugs all played a role in their preventable deaths. To me, the messages that other parents can learn from their lives are clear, and my hope is that in sharing their stories with readers, I will help parents help African American youth avoid the pitfalls that played a role in my brothers' deaths.

Why We Need to View and Treat African American Males Differently

Raising Black boys in a society that has always sought to destroy African American males is difficult, especially for single mothers. But raising them to become hard working, decent, law abiding citizens isn't impossible. Throughout history, countless African American parents, including single mothers, have done this. For parents, winning the war to save our Black boys must begin with adopting a different mindset about them. Instead of assuming that they will turn out badly, labeling them as "bad" at an early age, and thereby destroying their self-esteem in the home, we must build them up, believe in their potential to turn out well, and convince them that when God made them, He didn't make a mistake and He didn't make junk. They have a purpose to fulfill, and we must help

A Brighter Day:
How Parents Can Help African American Youth

them set and achieve realistic goals through our own words and deeds.

My brothers spent most of their childhood growing up on a cul-de-sac that only had nine houses on the street. Thirteen African American boys grew up on that tiny street. Two were murdered. Nine ended up serving one or more prison sentences. Three of the four who, to my knowledge, turned into decent men and escaped the prison pipeline, lived in two-parent homes and had positive male role models at home. But the boy, who became the most successful of the 13, grew up in a single-parent home. His mother, a nurse, struggled to raise her children to become law-abiding citizens, yet the prison pipeline trapped two of her sons when they were teens. Her youngest son could have followed in his older brothers' footsteps, but he chose a different path. He stayed out of trouble, took his education seriously, moved to another city, got a good paying job, married, and had children.

The last time that I saw him was at my brother Calvin's funeral. This man was the *only* person in the audience who stood up and found anything positive to say about his former friend who had become a notorious gang member. Instead of focusing on my brother's wasted potential, drug addiction, and criminal deeds, he chose to remember Calvin as his childhood friend—the little chocolate-colored boy who had so much potential. His words reminded me that my brother was a sensitive little boy who wasn't destined to spend time in prison or die violently. Like this neighbor from the single parent home who turned out well in life, my brother was destined for a better life, and so is every African American boy and girl. Let us keep this in mind as we parent, mentor, and prepare our youth, especially our boys, for adulthood. The prison pipeline can be avoided!

Chapter 7: How We Can Help Our Youth Avoid Prison Incarceration

A Final Word

Without a doubt, the United States justice system has a racist legacy that continues today. As I was writing this chapter, several cases surfaced about individuals who were freed from prison after having been wrongfully convicted. Many were Black males who lost irreplaceable years of their lives while they languished behind prison bars for crimes they didn't commit. Although the drug sentencing laws are being modified to eliminate disparities between the punishments given for crack cocaine-related offenses versus other types of drugs, the justice system still has many problems that have not been corrected.

One of the major problems involves the number of Black youth who get caught in the cradle-to-prison and school-to-prison pipelines early in life. We parents must do everything we can to keep our children and other family members from getting caught in these traps. However, because of the disproportionate number of talented and promising Black children who may one day end up in this horrible, unjust, and racist system, I want to end this chapter with additional advice for parents who find themselves dealing with the justice system:

- Hire the best attorney that you can afford. Public defenders are overworked and underpaid and usually don't have the resources that other attorneys have access to. According to the late Johnnie Cochran, "Money plays the most important role in the criminal justice system. . . ."[24] Although Cochran agreed that the justice system is racist, unfair, and has always treated Blacks worst than Whites, he believed strongly that money makes more of a difference than race. In fact, Cochran said that O. J. Simpson would've probably been convicted of murder if he'd been poor versus wealthy. Simpson's wealth allowed him to hire experienced, highly-reputable lawyers, and according to Cochran, this made the ultimate difference.

- We must teach our children that appearances matter. It's difficult enough to get a fair trial in the United States if a person is African American, but if the African American defendant is dressed inappropriately in court, that individual is going to have an even harder time getting a fair trial. Boys who look like thugs and gang members and girls who look promiscuous will, undoubtedly, make a negative impression on jurors. Once, when I was in a court waiting room, I witnessed this very situation. A Black teenager who had been charged with a crime was waiting to enter the courtroom. His hair was cornrowed, his pants were sagging, and I suspected that he was a gang member. When the bailiff called his case, the boy rose and a man who appeared to be his father followed. They looked like twins. The man's hair was cornrowed, his pants were sagging, and he looked like a thug himself. From the moment that they walked into the courtroom, I knew that their appearance would be used against them. Johnny Cochran confirmed that appearance can matter in the courtroom.[25] In my opinion, males should wear business suits or at least a shirt, dress slacks, and a tie to court. Females should be dressed as professionally as possible in a business suit or a dress that is not too tight or too short. Youth shouldn't chew gum. Parents should warn them ahead of time that they should be polite in court, never use profanity, and try to control their temper when they are being questioned.

- Don't believe everything you're told about your child's case. African American parents with limited finances will probably have to rely on public defenders to represent their children. As two attorneys recently reminded me, public defenders and prosecutors usually work closely together, sometimes even socialize together and often are paid by the same boss. Because of their limited resources and huge case loads, public defenders often try to get defendants to accept a plea bargain to a lesser charge, which might result in a lighter sentence. In many cases, this is not in the best interest of the defendant, especially one who is innocent. I know of numerous cases involving Black youth who ended up suffering and serving stiff sentences because a public defender pressured them to plea bargain. Before you allow your child to accept a plea bargain, you should weigh the pros and cons carefully, try to talk to other attorneys and individuals who are knowledgeable about the justice system, and get promises from attorneys in writing. (Black churches are a good place to find attorneys who might be willing to give advice.)

- African American parents should also consider signing up for a pre-paid legal plan before you even need it. These plans permit clients to pay monthly, affordable fees so that they can have access to legal representation when and if they ever need it. You can find more information about these plans on the Internet and in the telephone directory.

Conclusion: Loving Our Children Enough to Do the Right Thing

In order for African American youth to have a bright future, they need to be reared in loving homes. Every child needs and desires to be loved. But love isn't enough. A White teacher who teaches incarcerated juveniles once proved this point to me. "I meet parents all of the time who love their children," she explained. "But their children are locked up, and often it's because the parents made bad choices" Throughout the years, as I've thought about her statement, I've come to realize that it is true. That's why I'm saying that as African American parents, we have to do a lot more than merely love our children. We must love them enough to do the right things, the things that are in our children's best interests. So let me conclude by reminding you of some of the main points that I've tried to cover in this book:

- African American children need to be reared in loving homes in which they receive proper discipline—but not any form of physical, verbal, sexual, or emotional abuse.
- We must instill proper values and morals in our children, and provide them with a strong spiritual foundation.
- We parents should work on our own personal baggage on an ongoing basis.
- We must learn ways to build our children's self-esteem.
- We must help our children accept their physical features, skin tone, and hair.
- We must be diligent about helping our children achieve academic success, by ensuring that they develop strong

A Brighter Day:
How Parents Can Help African American Youth

reading, math, and writing skills, and that they are well behaved at school.

- We must equip our children with information and strategies that will enable them to deal wisely with law enforcement.
- We must be good role models.
- We must teach our children how to avoid the prison pipeline.
- We must teach our children how to deal with racism and discrimination.
- We must prepare our youth for the workforce, and teach them how to speak, dress, and behave at work.
- We must teach our youth important life lessons about dealing with rejection, toxic people, and forgiveness.

The recent historic presidential election that culminated with the inauguration of this nation's first Black president, Barack Obama, should give all African Americans hope. Our youth deserve to have big dreams of becoming president, doctors, attorneys, good parents, teachers, clergymen and women, politicians, business owners, real estate agents, honest law enforcement agents, bankers, college administrators, authors, radio and television hosts, and other good things.

As parents, it is our moral obligation to do everything that we can to increase our children's chances of having a bright future. When they have a bright future, our future as parents will be brighter, because we won't be visiting them in jail or raising grandchildren whose parents became dysfunctional because of bad choices that we made or generational cycles that we passed on.

I wish you well as you strive to ensure that your children and other African American youth will have a brighter day!

Bibliography

Introduction

1. DeBecker, G. (1997). *The Gift of Fear: Survival Signals That Protect Us From Violence*. Boston: Little, Brown and Company.
2. Ibid. p. 178.
3. Ibid. p. 179.
4. Forum on Child and Family Statistics. "America's Children in Brief: Key National Indicators of Well-Being, 2006." <http://www.childstats.gov/americaschildren/tables>. Tables Health 8.A & 8B. Retrieved October 10, 2006.
5. Ibid. Table ECON1-A. Retrieved October 10, 2006.
6. Ibid. Table HEALTH10. Retrieved October 10, 2006.
7. Ibid. Table POP6. Retrieved October 10, 2006.
8. Ibid. Table POP6.B. Retrieved October 10, 2006.
9. Benard, B. (2004). *Resiliency: What We Have Learned*. San Francisco: WestEd

Chapter 1

1. Violence Against Children Widely Accepted: U.N. study. MedlinePlus. <http://www.nlm.nih.gov/medlineplus>. Retrieved October 13, 2006.
2. Child Maltreatment 2001: Summary of Key Findings. Washington D.C. National
Clearinghouse on Child Abuse and Neglect Information. p. 1.
3. Centers for Disease Control. Child Maltreatment: Fact Sheet. <http:www.cdc.gov/ncipc/factsheets/cmfacts.htm>. Retrieved October 13, 2006.
4. Centers for Disease Control. ACE Study-Prevalence-Adverse Childhood Experiences. <http://apps.nccd.cdc.gov>. Retrieved October 13, 2006.

5. American Academy of Pediatrics Medical Library. Child Abuse and Neglect. <http://www.medem.com/MedLB>. Retrieved October 13, 2006.

6. Prevent Child Abuse America. Recognizing Child Abuse. What Parents Should Know. <www.preventchildabuse.org>. Retrieved October 13, 2006.

7. Centers for Disease Control. ACE Study-Prevalence-Adverse Childhood Experiences. <http://apps.nccd.cdc.gov>. Retrieved October 13, 2006.

8. Prevent Child Abuse America. Recognizing Child Abuse. What Parents Should Know. <www.preventchildabuse.org>. Retrieved October 13, 2006.

9. Centers for Disease Control. ACE Study-Prevalence-Adverse Childhood Experiences. <http://apps.nccd.cdc.gov>. Retrieved October 13, 2006.

10. Centers for Disease Control. Child Maltreatment: Overview. <http:www.cdc.gov/ncipc/factsheets/cmoverview.htm>. Retrieved October 13, 2006.

11. Childabuse.com. Indications of Child Abuse & Maltreatment. <http://www.childabuse.com/help.htm>. Retrieved October 13, 2006.

12. Centers for Disease Control. Child Maltreatment: Fact Sheet. <http:www.cdc.gov/ncipc/factsheets/cmfacts.htm>. Retrieved October 13, 2006.

13. Centers for Disease Control. Child Maltreatment: Overview. <http:www.cdc.gov/ncipc/factsheets/cmoverview.htm>. Retrieved October 13, 2006.

14. Childabuse.com. Indications of Child Abuse & Maltreatment. <http://www.childabuse.com/help.htm>. Retrieved October 13, 2006.

Bibliography

15. Centers for Disease Control. ACE Study-Prevalence-Adverse Childhood Experiences. <http://apps.nccd.cdc.gov>. Retrieved October 13, 2006.

16. Childabuse.com. Indications of Child Abuse & Maltreatment. <http://www.childabuse.com/help.htm>. Retrieved October 13, 2006.

17. USA Today. (October 5, 2006). Pedophile Priest Confesses in Documentary. <http://usatoday.com>. Retrieved October 28, 2006.

18. Los Angeles Times. (October 6, 2006). Former Thousand Oaks Pastor Held in Molestation. <http://latimes.com>. Retrieved October 28, 2006.

19. The Sacramento Bee. (October 16, 2006). San Diego Nurse Sentenced to 14 Years for Molesting Patient. <http://www.sacbee.com>. Retrieved October 28, 2006.

20. Ibid.

21. Fox News.com. (October 26, 2003). Couple Arrested on Charges of Starving Kids. <http://www.foxnews.com>. Retrieved October 29, 2006.

22. Washington County Sheriff's Office Media Information. (July 22, 2004). Foster Parent Arrested for Sexually Abusing Children in His Care. <http://www.co.washington.or.us/sheriff/media/fostabus.htm>. Retrieved October 29, 2006.

23. lasvegasnow.com. (October 23, 2006). Foster Mom Arrested in Baby Charles Case. <http://www.klas-tv.com/global/story>. Retrieved October 29, 2006.

24. U. S. Department of Health & Human Services. *Child Maltreatment 2004*. <http:www.acf.hhs.gov/programs/cb/pubs/cm04/chapterthree.htm>. Retrieved October 29, 2006.

25. CNN.com. (February 5, 2005). Pair Accused of Child Torture Arrested in Utah. Florida Officials Say 5 of 7 Children

Suffered Starvation, Abuse. <http://cnn.usnews>. Retrieved October 29, 2006.

26. CNN.com. (May 5, 2005). Mother, Stepfather Charged in "Precious Doe" Killing. Tipster Provides Name of Girl Found Decapitated in 2001.

27. Childabuse.com. Why Child Abuse Occurs & the Common Criminal Background of the Abuser. <http://www.childabuse.com/perp.htm>. Retrieved October 13, 2006.

28. Ibid.

29. Ibid.

30. Ibid.

31. Ibid.

32. Ibid.

33. Bethea, L.. (March 15, 1999). Primary Prevention of Child Abuse. American Family Physician. <http://www.aafp.org/afp/990315ap/1577.html>. Retrieved November 1, 2006.

34. Public Health Agency of Canada National Celaringhouse on Family Violence. Child Abuse and Neglect Overview Paper.
<http://www.phac-aspc.gc.ca/ncfv-cnivf/familyviolence/html/nfntsnegle.html>. Retrieved November 1, 2006.

35. Centers for Disease Control and Prevention. Adverse Childhood Experiences Study. Major Findings. <http://www.cdc.gov/NCCDPHP/ACE/findings.htm>. Retrieved October 13, 2006.

36. Morrison, H. & Goldberg, H. (2004). *My Life Among the Serial Killers*: *Inside the Minds of the World's Most Notorious Murderers*. p. 26. New York: HarperCollins Publishers.

37. Ibid.

38. Ibid.

39. Salter, A. (2004). *Predators: Pedophiles, Rapists, and Other Sex Offenders*. NY: Basic Books.

Bibliography

40. Stout, M. (2005). *The Sociopath Next Door.* New York: Broadway Books.

41. Magid, K. & McKelvey, C. A. (1987). *High Risk: Children Without a Conscience.* New York: Bantam Books.

42. Ibid

43. Scott, S. L. Mary Bell. CourtTV Crime Library. <http://www.crimelibrary.com>. Retrieved November 5, 2006.

44. Gibbs, N. R. (September 19, 1994). Murder in Miniature. Time. <http://www.time.com/time/magazine>. Retrieved November 5, 2006.

45. Children's Defense Fund. Child Abuse and Neglect. <http://www.childrensdefense.org>.
Retrieved November 5, 2006.

46. Childhelp. Child Abuse in America. <http://www.childhelpusa.org/resources/learning-center/statistics>. Retrieved November 5, 2006.

47. ACLU. Words from Prison-Did You Know…? <http://www.aclu.org>. Retrieved November 5, 2006.

48. Magid, K. & McKelvey, C. A. (1987). *High Risk: Children Without a Conscience.* New York: Bantam Books.

49. McClurkin, D. (2001). *Eternal Victim, Eternal Victor.* Lanham, MD: Pneuma Life Publishing.

50. Tavis Smiley. About the Show. <http://www.pbs.org/kcet/tavissmiley>. Retrieved November 13, 2006.

51. Ibid.

52. Johnson, P. K. (March, 2006). Diary of a Brilliant Black Man. *Essence* pp. 120-123.

53. Jones, Q. (2001). *The Autobiography of Quincy Jones.* New York: Random House.

54. Ibid.

55. Fisher, A. Q. (2001). *Finding Fish: A Memoir.* New York: Perennial.

A Brighter Day:
How Parents Can Help African American Youth

56. HarperCollins. Author Interview: Antwone Q. Fisher on *Finding Fish.*

57. The Time 100. <http://www.time.com/time/time100/artists/profile/winfrey2.html>. Retrieved November 15, 2006.

58. Ibid

59. Academy of Achievement. Biography: Maya Angelou. <http://www.achievement.org>. Retrieved November 15, 2006.

60. Smithsonian Magazine. (2003). A Conversation with Maya Angelou at 75. <http://www.smithsonianmagazine.com/issues/2003/april/angelou.htm>. Retrieved November 15, 2006.

61. Academy of Achievement. Biography: Maya Angelou. <http://www.achievement.org>. Retrieved November 15, 2006.

62. Houghton Mifflin Reading: Meet the Author: Maya Angelou. <http://www.eduplace.com/kids/tnc/mtai/angelou.html>. Retrieved November 15, 2006.

63. Comer, J. P. & Poussaint, A. F. (1992). *Raising Black Children: Two Leading Psychiatrists Confront the Educational, Social and Emotional Problems Facing Black Children.* New York: New York: Plume.

64. Bethea, L. American Family Physician. Primary Prevention of Child Abuse. The American Academy of Family Physicians. <http://www.aafp.org/afp/990315ap/1577.html>. Retrieved November 1, 2006.

65. Magid, K. & McKelvey, C. A. (1987). *High Risk: Children Without a Conscience.* New York: Bantam Books.

66. Crain, W. (1992). *Theories of Development: Concepts and Applications* (3rd edition). Englewood Cliffs, NJ: Prentice Hall, Inc.

Bibliography

67. Centers for Disease Control. Positive Parenting Tips for Healthy Child Development: Infants (0-1 year old). <www.cdc.gov/ncbdd>. Retrieved November 23, 2006.

68. Ibid.

69. Centers for Disease Control. Positive Parenting Tips for Healthy Child Development: Toddlers (2-3 years old). <www.cdc.gov/ncbdd>. Retrieved November 23, 2006.

70. Ibid.

71. Comer, J. P. & Poussaint, A. F. (1992). *Raising Black Children: Two Leading Psychiatrists Confront the Educational, Social and Emotional Problems Facing Black Children*. New York: New York: Plume.

72. Centers for Disease Control. Positive Parenting Tips for Healthy Child Development: Preschoolers (3-5 years old). <www.cdc.gov/ncbdd>. Retrieved November 23, 2006.

73. Comer, J. P. & Poussaint, A. F. (1992). *Raising Black Children: Two Leading Psychiatrists Confront the Educational, Social and Emotional Problems Facing Black Children*. New York: New York: Plume.

74. Centers for Disease Control. Positive Parenting Tips for Healthy Child Development: Middle Childhood (9-11 years old). <www.cdc.gov/ncbdd>. Retrieved November 23, 2006.

75. Comer, J. P. & Poussaint, A. F. (1992). *Raising Black Children: Two Leading Psychiatrists Confront the Educational, Social and Emotional Problems Facing Black Children*. New York: New York: Plume.

76. Centers for Disease Control. Positive Parenting Tips for Healthy Child Development: Preschoolers (3-5 years old). <www.cdc.gov/ncbdd>. Retrieved November 23, 2006.

77. Kunjufu, J. (1984). *Developing Positive Self-Images & Discipline in Black Children*. Chicago: African American Images.

78. Kunjufu, J. (1990). *Countering the Conspiracy to Destroy Black Boys Vol. lll.* Chicago: African American Images.

79. Ibid.

80. Ibid.

81. Comer, J. P. & Poussaint, A. F. (1992). *Raising Black Children: Two Leading Psychiatrists Confront the Educational, Social and Emotional Problems Facing Black Children.* New York: New York: Plume.

82. Smiley, T. & Ritz, D. (2006). *What I Know for Sure*: *My Story of Growing Up in America.* New York: Doubleday.

83. Elder Abuse and Neglect: In Search of Solutions. (2006). American Psychological Association. <http://www.apa.org/pi/aging/eldabuse.html>. Retrieved November 15, 2006.

84. National Clearinghouse on Abuse in Later Life. <http://www.ncall.us/>. Retrieved November 15, 2006.

85. Ibid.

86. Heide, K. (September, 1992). Why Kids Kill Parents. *Psychology Today.* <http://www.psychologytoday.com>. Retrieved November 15, 2006.

87. Ibid

88. Ibid

89. Elder Abuse and Neglect: In Search of Solutions. (2006). American Psychological Association. <http://www.apa.org/pi/aging/eldabuse.html>. Retrieved November 15, 2006.

Chapter 2

1. Hooks, B. (2003). *Rock My Soul: Black People and Self-Esteem.* New York: Atria Books.

2. Branden, N. (1997). What Self-Esteem is and is Not. <http://www.nathanielbranden.com/catalog/articles_essays/what_self_e...>. Retrieved December 23, 2006.

3. Reasoner, R. The True Meaning of Self-Esteem. P. 1. <http://www.self-esteem-nase.org/whatisselfesteem.shtml>. Retrieved December 23, 2006.

4. Ibid.

5. Hooks, B. (2003). *Rock My Soul: Black People and Self-Esteem*. New York: Atria Books.

6. Reasoner, R. The True Meaning of Self-Esteem. P. 1. <http://www.self-esteem-nase.org/whatisselfesteem.shtml>. Retrieved December 23, 2006. p. 1. <http://www.washingtonpost.com/wp-dyn/content/article/2005/07/24/AR2005072401115.html.7>.

7. Raspberry, W. (July 25, 2005). Why Our Black Families Are Failing. Washington Post. <http://www.washingtonpost.com/wpdyn/content/article/2005/07/24/AR2005072401115.html>. p. 1.

8. King James Version of the Bible. Genesis 9:20–25.

9. McGee, J. V. (1981). *Thru the Bible with J. Vernon McGee*. (Volume 1: Genesis-Deuteronomy). Pasadena, CA: Thru the Bible Radio. p. 49

10. Ibid. p. 51.

11. Carson, B. (1999). *The Big Picture: Getting Perspective on What's Really Important in Life*. Grand Rapids, Michigan: Zondervan Publishing House.

Chapter 3 Racism

1. Boyd-Franklin, N. (2003). *Black Families in Therapy: Understanding the African American Experience*. (Second Edition). New York: The Guilford Press.

2. Levin, A. (December 15, 2006). Battling Depression Among Blacks Means Confronting Racism's Legacy. *Psychiatric News*. Vol. 41, No. 24, p. 4. <http://pn.psychiatryonline.org/cgi/content/full/41/24/4-a>. Retrieved November 15, 2006.

A Brighter Day:
How Parents Can Help African American Youth

3. Lucy D. Suddreth, (1993). How Racism Affects Everyone: Alvin Poussaint Delivers Keynote Address. <http://www.loc.gov/loc/lcib/93/9304/racism.html>. Retrieved November 15, 2006.

4. Boyd-Franklin, N. (2003). *Black Families in Therapy: Understanding the African American Experience.* (Second Edition). New York: The Guilford Press.

5. Comer, J. P. & Poussaint, A. F. (1992). *Raising Black Children: Two Leading Psychiatrists Confront the Educational, Social and Emotional Problems Facing Black Children.* New York: New York: Plume. p. 17.

6. Ibid.

7. Thompson, G. L. (2002). *African American Teens Discuss Their Schooling Experiences.* Westport, CT: Praeger; Thompson, G. L. (2007). *Up Where We Belong: Helping African American and Latino Students Rise in School and in Life.* San Francisco: Jossey Bass.

8. Thompson, G. L. (1998). *Predictors of Resilience in African American Adults.* Unpublished Doctoral Dissertation. Claremont, CA: The Claremont Graduate University.

9. Thompson, G. L. (2003). *What African American Parents Want Educators to Know.* Westport, CT: Greenwood Publishers.

10. Wing Sue, D. (2003). *Overcoming Our Racism: The Journey to Liberation.* San Francisco: Jossey Bass.

11. Ibid.

12. Bonilla-Silva, E. (2003). *Racism Without Racists: Color-Blind Racism and the Persistence of Racial Inequality in the United States.* Lanham, MD: Rowman & Littlefield Publishers, Inc.

13. Wing Sue, D. (2003). *Overcoming Our Racism: The Journey to Liberation.* San Francisco: Jossey Bass.

Bibliography

14. De Becker, G. (1997). *The Gift of Fear: Survival Signals that Protect Us From Violence*. Boston: Little, Brown and Company. pp. 17 & 73.

15. Wing Sue, D. (2003). *Overcoming Our Racism: The Journey to Liberation*. San Francisco: Jossey Bass. p. 262.

16. Ibid

17. Ibid.

18. Bell, C. (2004). Racism: A Mental Illness? PSYCHIATRIC SERVICES December 2004 Vol. 55 No. 12. <http://psychservices.psychiatryonline.org/cgi/reprint/55/12/1343>. Retrieved February 25, 2007.

19. Ibid.

20. Carter, K. L. (2006). Finding the Reasons for Prejudices: Psychiatrists Debating Whether Racism is a Social, Mental Illness. The Philadelphia Tribune. <http://www.phila-tribune.com/channel/inthenews/012807/racism.asp>. Retrieved February 25, 2007. p. 1.

21. Eakin, E. (January 15, 2000). Bigotry as Mental Illness or Just Another Norm. The New York Times. <http://query.nytimes.com/gst/fullpage.html?sec=health&res=9A01E1D9 133AF936A25752C0A9669C8B63&n= Retrieved February 25, 2007. p. 2.

22. Bell, C. (2004). Racism: A Mental Illness? PSYCHIATRIC SERVICES December 2004 Vol. 55 No. 12. <http://psychservices.psychiatryonline.org/cgi/reprint/55/12/1343>. Retrieved February 25, 2007.

23. Carter, K. L. (2006). Finding the Reasons for Prejudices: Psychiatrists Debating Whether Racism is a Social, Mental Illness. The Philadelphia Tribune. <http://www.phila-tribune.com/channel/inthenews/012807/racism.asp>. Retrieved February 25, 2007. p. 2.

24. Ibid. p. 2.

25. Bonilla-Silva, E. (2003). *Racism Without Racists: Color-Blind Racism and the Persistence of Racial Inequality in the United States*. Lanham, MD: Rowman & Littlefield Publishers, Inc.

26. U.S. Census Bureau. (2003). Married-couple and Unmarried-Partner Households: 2000: Census 2000 Special Reports. <http://www.census.gov/prod/2003pubs/censr-5.pdf>. Retrieved February 25, 2007.

27. Thompson, G. L. (2007). *Up Where We Belong: Helping African American and Latino Students Rise in School and in Life*. San Francisco: Jossey Bass.

28. Comer, J. P. & Poussaint, A. F. (1992). *Raising Black Children: Two Leading Psychiatrists Confront the Educational, Social and Emotional Problems Facing Black Children*. New York: New York: Plume.

29. Kochman, T. (1981). *Black and White Styles in Conflict*. Chicago: The University of Chicago Press.

30. Braiker, H. B. (2001). *The Disease to Please: Curing the People-Pleasing Syndrome*. New York: McGraw Hill, p. 7.

31. Ibid.

Chapter 4

1. Richardson, C. Toxic Relationships: The People. <http://www.oprah.com/spiritself/lybl/control/ss_lybl_control_10_b.jhtml>. Retrieved March 27, 2007. P. 1.

2. Ibid., p. 1.

3. Ibid., p. 1.

4. Ibid., p. 1.

Bibliography

5. Salter, A. (2004). *Predators, Pedophiles, Rapists, and Other Sex Offenders: Who They Are, How they Operate, and How We Can Protect Ourselves and Our Children*. New York: Basic Books.

6. Pirisi, A. (December 13, 2006). Forgive to Live. *Psychology Today*. <http://psychologytoday.com/rss/index.php?term=pto-20000701-000025& print=1>. Retrieved April 15, 2007.

7. The Power of Forgiveness, Forgive Others: Five Reasons to Learn to Forgive. (January, 2005*). Harvard Women's Health Watch*. <http://www.health.harvard.edu/press_releases/power_of_forgiveness.htm>. Retrieved April 15, 2007.

8. Asher, S. R. & Williams, G. (1993). Children Without Friends. In Todd, C.M. (Ed.), *Day Care Center Connections*, 2(26). National Network for Child Care-NNCC. <http://www.nncc.org/Guidance/dc26_wo.friends1.html>. Retrieved April 21, 2007. p.2.

9. Ibid. p. 2.

10. Ibid. pp. 3–6.

11. The Earth Times. Health News Editor. (2007). Art Therapy Helps Traumatized Children. <http://www.earthtimes.org/articles/show/25932.html>. Retrieved April 28, 2007.

12. Cosentino, B. W. (2005). Art Therapy: How Creative Expression Can Heal. <http://healthgate.partners.org/browsing/Content.asp?fileName>. Retrieved April 28, 2007.

13. Thompson, G. L. (1998).). *Predictors of Resilience in African-American Adults*. Unpublished Doctoral Dissertation. The Claremont Graduate University, p. 58.

14. Ibid. p. 69.

15. Carson, B. (1999). *The Big Picture: Getting Perspective on What's Really Important in Life*. Grand Rapids, Michigan: Zondervan Publishing House.

16. Brown, T. (2003). *What Mama Taught Me: The Seven Core Values of Life*. New York: William Morrow.

Chapter 5

1. Ferguson, A. A. (2001). *Bad Boys: Public Schools in the Making of Black Masculinity*. Ann Arbor: University of Michigan Press.

2. Markow, D. & Martin, S. (2005). *The MetLife Survey of the American Teacher: Transitions and the Role of Supportive Relationships, A Survey of Teachers, Principals and Students*. Warwick, RI.: MetLife; U. S. Department of Education (2003). Getting Ready to Pay for College: What Students and Their Parents Know about the Cost of College Tuition and What They are Doing to Find Out. Washington, DC: Institute of Education Sciences.

3. National PTA/Building Successful Partnerships. Benefits of Parent Involvement. Tab 6. Handout 1. <www.wastatepta.org/resources/parent_outreach/research_findings.pdf>. Retrieved May 22, 2007.

4. Kunjufu, J. (1984). *Developing Positive Self-Images & Discipline in Black Children*. Chicago: African American Images.

5. Kunjufu, J. (1988). *To Be Popular or Smart: The Black Peer Group*. Chicago: African American Images.

6. U. S. Census Bureau. (n.d.) *The Big Payoff: Educational Attainment and Synthetic Estimates of Work-Life Earnings*. <http://www.census.gov/prod/2002 pubs/p23-210.pdf>. Retrieved December 13, 2006.

7. U. S. Census Bureau (September, 1997a). America's Children at Risk. Washington, D.C. U.S. Department of Commerce: Economics and Statistics Administration; U. S.

Bibliography

Census Bureau (September, 1997b). Children with Single Parents: How They Fare. Washington, D.C. U.S. Department of Commerce: Economics and Statistics Administration.

8. Cochran, J. & Fisher, D. (2002). *A Lawyer's Life*. New York: Thomas Dunne Books.

9. Franklin, J. H. (2005). *Mirror to America: The Autobiography of John Hope Franklin*.
New York: Farrar, Straus, and Giroux.

10. Henderson, S. (June, 2007). The Pursuit of Life After Prison. *Ebony*, pp. 130–134.

11. Mathis, G. (2002). *Inner City Miracle*. New York: One World/Ballantine.

Chapter 6

1. Pobojewski, S. (June 11, 1996). Etiquette in the Workplace is Still Important. The University Record. <http://www.umich.edu/~urecord/9596/Jun11_96/artcl17.htm>. Retrieved June 26, 2007.

2. Business ~ Workplace Etiquette: Job Interview Tips 101. The Emily Post Institute. <http://www.emilypost.com/business/interviews.htm>. Retrieved July 1, 2007.

3. Business ~ Workplace Etiquette: Tips on Making a Good First Impression. <http://www.emilypost.com/business/first_impression.htm>. Retrieved July 1, 2007, p. 1.

4. Business ~ Workplace Etiquette: Job Interview Tips 101. The Emily Post Institute. <http://www.emilypost.com/business/interviews.htm>. Retrieved July 1, 2007.

5. Business ~ Workplace Etiquette: Tips on Making a Good First Impression. <http://www.emilypost.com/business/first_impression.htm>. Retrieved July 1, 2007, p. 1.

6. Ibid. p. 1.

A Brighter Day:
How Parents Can Help African American Youth

7. Race/Color Discrimination. The U. S. Equal Employment Opportunity Commission. <http://www.eeoc.gov/types/race.html>. Retrieved July 2, 2007.

Chapter 7

1. Ventura, J. (1996). *Law for Dummies: A Reference for the Rest of Us!* Indianapolis, Indiana: Wiley.
2. Cochran, J. & Fisher, D. (2002). *A Lawyer's Life*. New York: Thomas Dunne Books.
3. Ibid. p. 15.
4. Durose, M. R., Smith, E., Langan, P. (April, 2007). Bureau of Justice Statistics Special Report: Contacts Between Police and the Public, 2005. Washington, DC: U. S. Department of Justice, Office of Justice Programs, p. 1.
5. Ibid. p. 4.
6. Chideya, F. (1995). *Don't Believe the Hype: Fighting Cultural Misinformation about African-Americans*. New York: Plume.
7. Harris, D. A. (June, 1999). Driving While Black: Racial Profiling On Our Nation's Highways. ACLU. <http://www.aclu.org/racialjustice/racialprofiling/15912pub1999 0607.html>. Retrieved September 4, 2007, p. 3.
8. Juveniles and Drugs. Drug Facts. Office of National Drug Control Policy. <http://www.whitehousedrugpolicy.gov/drugfact/juveniles/index.html>. Retrieved September 17, 2007.
9. Ibid. p. 3.
10. Crack. Drug Facts: Office of National Drug Control Policy. <http://www.whitehousedrugpolicy.gov/drugfact/crack/index.html>. Retrieved September 17, 2007.

Bibliography

11. Ibid. p. 3.

12. Drug Use. U. S. Department of Justice Office of Justice Programs. <http://www.ojp.usdoj.gov/bjs/dcf/du.htm>. p. 4. Retrieved September 12, 2007.

13. Juveniles and Drugs. Drug Facts. Office of National Drug Control Policy. <http://www.whitehousedrugpolicy.gov/drugfact/juveniles/index.html>. Retrieved September 17, 2007. p. 4.

14. Ibid. p. 2.

15. Sentencing Children to Die in Prison. Equal Justice Initiative. Montgomery, Alabama. <www.eji.org>. Retrieved November 20, 2007.

16. Ibid. p. 1.

17. Child Abuse And Neglect. The Children's Defense Fund. <http://www.childrensdefense.org/site/PageServer?pagename=Programs_Cradle_Abuse_Neglect>. Retrieved December 3, 2007.

18. Ibid.

19. Ibid.

20. Ibid.

21. American Civil Liberties Union: School to Prison Pipeline-An Overview. <http://www.aclu.org/crimjustice/juv/24704res20060321.html>. Retrieved December 12, 2007. p.1.

22. Dismantling the School-to-Prison Pipeline. NAACP Legal Defense and Educational Fund, Inc. <http://www.naacpldf.org/issues.aspx?issue=3>. Retrieved December 12, 2007. p.2.

23. Ibid. p. 4.

24. Cochran, J. & Fisher, D. (2002). *A Lawyer's Life*. New York: Thomas Dunne Books.

25. Ibid.

A Brighter Day:
How Parents Can Help African American Youth

Notes

_____

_____

_____

_____

_____

_____

_____

_____

_____

_____

_____

_____

_____

_____

_____

_____

_____

_____

_____

_____

_____

Notes

Notes

A Brighter Day:
How Parents Can Help African American Youth

Notes

_____

_____

_____

_____

_____

_____

_____

_____

_____

_____

_____

_____

_____

_____

_____

_____

_____

_____

_____

_____

_____

_____

_____

Notes

A Brighter Day:
How Parents Can Help African American Youth

Notes

_____

_____

_____

_____

_____

_____

_____

_____

_____

_____

_____

_____

_____

_____

_____

_____

_____

_____

_____

_____

_____

_____

Notes

Notes

_____

_____

_____

_____

_____

_____

_____

_____

_____

_____

_____

_____

_____

_____

_____

_____

_____

_____

_____

_____

_____

_____

_____

A Brighter Day:
How Parents Can Help African American Youth

Notes

_____

_____

_____

_____

_____

_____

_____

_____

_____

_____

_____

_____

_____

_____

_____

_____

_____

_____

_____

_____

_____

_____